The NEW Office

Designs for Corporations, People & Technology

KARIN TETLOW

Architecture and Interior Design

AN IMPRINT OF
PBC INTERNATIONAL, INC.

Distributor to the book trade in the United States and Canada
Rizzoli International Publications
through St. Martin's Press
300 Park Avenue South
New York, NY 10010

Distributor to the art trade in the United States and Canada
PBC International, Inc.
One School Street
Glen Cove, NY 11542

Distributor throughout the rest of the world
Hearst Books International
1350 Avenue of the Americas
New York, NY 10019

Library of Congress Cataloging–in–Publication Data
Tetlow, Karin
The new office: designs for corporations, people & technology /
    by Karin Tetlow
        p.   cm.
    Includes index.
    ISBN 0–86636–442–0 (alk. paper) ISBN 0-86636-497-8 (alk. paper)
    1. Offices—Designs and plans. 2. Interior architecture. 3. Office decoration.
    I. Title
NA6230.T45   1996
725'.2—dc20   96–16250
                                  CIP

CAVEAT– Information in this text is believed accurate, and will pose no
problem for the student or casual reader. However, the author was often
constrained by information contained in signed release forms, information
that could have been in error or not included at all. Any misinformation
(or lack of information) is the result of failure in these attestations. The
author has done whatever is possible to insure accuracy.

Designed by Karin Martin

Color separation, printing and binding by Dai Nippon Group

10 9 8 7 6 5 4 3 2 1

Printed in Hong Kong

I dedicate this book to my children Sam and Georgia
and to my mentors and friends in Five Element Acupuncture

Contents

Foreword

....

AESTHETICS AND COST MAY HAVE BEEN THE CORNERSTONES FOR THE WORKPLACE of the last two decades, but design of the workplace for the nineties is dictated by a number of additional elements. Any business, no matter its location, is facing a staggering list of challenges: rapid technological developments; increasingly complex and more costly environmental concerns; flexibility to accommodate re-configured work teams; sustainable design measures; employee concerns (ergonomics, ambiance, day care); fierce world-wide competition; dramatically shorter schedules; customers demanding more services and quality products at the lowest prices; the changing workforce; and global politics. These forces of change are affecting not only the way people work, but also how office environments are planned and designed. Clients are turning increasingly to designers to create a framework in which they can succeed in today's business world. Perhaps, as designers, our biggest challenge is learning to truly interface with our clients, to understand their businesses, and to form a partnership with them in order to most accurately meet their facilities' needs. Designers should focus on finding out what clients need and then on developing the strategies to deliver the services which meet those needs.

Designers are also having to re-think how the workplace is designed. We are learning how to integrate design, technology, data and service to create a business insight. Technology is important, design and production are critical, but understanding the client's business is essential. This is especially true as companies continue to look for ways not only to downsize and consolidate operations, but also to take advantage of new technologies and make employees more productive. Clients are demanding an inherent flexibility to allow for changing staff, size, projects, and cultures, all of which are greatly enhanced and facilitated by the use of new technology. More companies are consolidating specific elements of their operations, while relocating support staff and functions to decentralized, less expensive sites.

Companies will be incorporating more amenities (child care centers, fitness areas, cafeterias) into their office environments in order to attract the right staff and for recruitment at college campuses. However we label the transformation—re-engineering, reinventing, reorganization, downsizing or right sizing—these new strategies provide designers with opportunities to work very closely with clients to maximize use of their space. We find companies most effectively use space not only through efficient manipulation of space, but through comprehensive analysis of work needs, social needs, and careful monitoring of space utilization.

Studies have shown that workers are actually out of their workplaces a good deal of the time—on the road, in meetings, or on site with clients. The traditional nine-to-five work structure is no longer predominant, and the day of the contract worker, independent consultant, part-time employee prevails. As a result, the traditional work environment—single-occupancy workstations and private offices—is giving way to a number of alternative work environments to accommodate hoteling, telecommuting, etc. The reality is that people still want to work together in a community, to collaborate, and to produce. Therefore, in the end, clients tend to focus more on creating specific areas for different acitivities: project rooms, quiet rooms, guest areas, as well as collaborative environments that promote team-oriented work and facilitate interaction among employees. But, the vision of an office environment that only accommodates transitory workers will not be a reality in the immediate future.

Any business today must use all available resources—time, people, space, money, information, technology—to their fullest potential. Clients must be educated on the benefits of good office design and planning in order to help them see that just cutting costs will not make companies more competitive. A designer's work must exemplify one reality: good design can have a direct impact on a company by increasing productivity, adding value to the organization, and enhancing the environment and personal well-being of employees.

Antony Harbour, IIDA
Vice President, Managing Director, London

Gensler . . . *Architecture, Design & Planning Worldwide*

Introduction

OFFICES OF TODAY ARE THE HUBS OF OUR INFORMATION-DRIVEN WORLD. Equipped with fast-changing technology which makes time zones and geography irrelevant, they link a global economy and serve as workplaces for millions of people. They offer an anchor in a society increasingly on the move in cyberspace and elsewhere. Sometimes a comfy base to counteract the stress of technology, at other times a cacophony of colors, the office of the nineties is a place of unusual creativity. Smaller than the mega-projects of the eighties, they are expressions of a new expertise which relies on innovation rather than tradition and the transparent luxury of rich materials.

Whether the address was an exclusive chocolate house in seventeenth-century London or a high-rise cathedral to commerce built at the turn of the century, the office has long been more than simply a place of work. It was, and is, marketplace, image-maker, and metaphor for business goals. Its identity expressed in location, architecture, layout and furnishings, the office sends unmistakable messages to employees, clients and customers. The gothic-style paneling and hand-tooled Moroccan leather of New York's Woolworth building and the aged 98-year-old board room at MetLife awe visitors to this day. In contrast, present day interiors communicate more contemporary messages of excellence, flexibility and cost consciousness.

Yet it is as a place of work that the office has generated most attention since the turn of the century, when scientific management advocated regimentation of highly supervised workers seated in neat rows toiling at their adding machines. By the end of the eighties, most workers sat in individual cubicles and the expense of offices was second only to salaries and benefits. Officing had become very big business as consultants advised on the impact of office design and manufacturers sold millions of dollars of mostly the same free-standing "systems" furniture. Meanwhile, environmental and social consciousness grew along with knowledge of endangered wood species, the discovery of sick building syndrome brought about by deficient air circulation and toxic off-gassing from furnishings, and the passing of the Americans with Disabilities Act.

Then came the convergence of accessible technology with a tightening global market. Merger mania and corporate downsizing resulted in white collar layoffs in the millions since the early nineties. Networked computers on virtually every desk meant that office assistants could know as much as their immediate bosses and layers of management became redundant. Investment in computerization boomed and employers argued for new strategies—later named alternative officing, or AO—to reduce office costs by providing less space in their new down-sized quarters and to enhance performance. AO includes "hoteling" and "free address" for salespeople and consultants usually in the field, and "caves and commons" for project team members who need private and community spaces for solitary tasks and "teaming." Other options are telecommuting from home or satellite office and work anytime, anywhere in the "virtual office" using lap-tops and cell phones. Perhaps not unexpectedly, the most innovative AO has appeared in the creative sector where advertising agencies have commissioned striking new environments of team zones and wheelabout workstations.

The International Facility Management Association reports that 83 percent of companies are embracing AO. While we wait for research on its pleasures and pitfalls, serious questions are arising as to its long-term impact on our work-oriented culture, especially for those who seldom work in the office. On the corporate front, workers report an erosion of bonding with colleagues and losses of informal mentoring while on the personal side, many feel alienation, isolation and find difficulty drawing a boundary between home and work.

Meanwhile, the speedily-built offices of the late nineties catch the breath and spark the mind as each serves a multitude of complex roles. Refreshed by consciousness, challenged by budgetary limitations and driven to solve the practicalities of boosting performance, they lead the world in office design.

Karin Tetlow

Office as Marketplace

SINCE THE TIME OF MARKET DAYS when shoppers scrutinized each stall searching for the very best, sellers have known that presentation has to be just right. So it is with the office. Whether the item be product or service, Fred Flintstone, investment management or architectural expertise, appropriate visual presentation is crucial.

Professional display and a correct address are core ingredients, but the designer's true talent lies in identifying and translating into three-dimensional space the exact nature of what is being sold. In these days of sophisticated marketing, this is more likely to be concept and aspiration than mere product or service. Hence the themes of outdoor modernity for G.H. Bass and "back home" of the American Trade Center in Moscow.

The following offices range from the spectacular to the serious. Including The Design Collective's "learning laboratory" set in the heart of a shopping mall, California ambiance for Credit Lyonnais and an iconoclastic showroom for Betsey Johnson's fashion flair, they are prime examples of the contemporary office as marketplace.

Betsey Johnson Showroom

Fashion Design

Betsey Johnson clothes have their own distinct character, which is very much part of the persona of Betsey Johnson. So when she decided on new headquarters and showroom in the heart of New York City's bustling garment district, she chose a design firm which understood her unconventional and iconoclastic flair for mixing color and shape. Tarik Currimbhoy Design & Architecture had recently completed her apartment and knew how to translate her image into a three-dimensional functional space by delivering a skeleton floorplan and built-ins and leaving the rest to Betsey.

Breaking all design school rules regarding the need for a consistent conceptual scheme, she co-mingles bright ochers and hot pinks, and places a 70s table next to a gilded chair. The antiques are an eclectic marvel picked up piece by piece. Currimbhoy assisted with the lighting, floor finishes and custom office furniture.

The heart of the 12,000 square foot space located in New York City's frenzied garment center is the showroom. Buyers stepping off the elevator and entering through a small reception and lobby immediately experience the impact of

LOCATION: New York, New York **ARCHITECT:** Tarik Currimbhoy Design & Architecture **INTERIOR DESIGNER:** Betsey Johnson **SIZE:** 12,000 square feet **COST:** $40/ square foot **PHOTOGRAPHY:** Peter Paige

the colorful eccentric space. The checkerboard flooring and steel doors serve as an ideal hard-edged backdrop for Betsey's eccentric choices and murals which she painted herself.

LIGHTING: Lightlab, Abolite by Continental Lighting; PAINT: Benjamin Moore; CARPENTRY: custom by Brito Builders; FLOORING: Town & Country; ANTIQUES: Geffner and Schatzy; CONTRACTOR: Excel Construction

G.H. Bass & Co.

Regional Sales Office

The G.H. Bass sales office is more than a flexible home base for sales representatives of one of America's best known shoe manufacturers. It redefines a famous name with an updated look better suited to a younger generation of buyers and new ways of doing business with portable technology. Employing a mixture of scales and references, New York design firm Parsons + Fernandez-Casteleiro organized the full floor around a grid generated by the periphery wall and large views towards Central Park. Enclosed, non-assigned offices are located on the perimeter wall and share computer and telecommunications connections, while administrative and storage support are located in the central core. The flexible common area is divided by sliding partitions and translucent and movable walls according to the need for large gatherings or small informal meetings. Traditional materials of maple, natural canvas and leather were deliberately specified to echo the long established Maine-based Bass reputation.

PAINT: Benjamin Moore, Pratt & Lambert; SLATE FLOORING: P.M. Cousins; CERAMIC TILES: American Olean; CARPET TILES: Lees; FLOOR STRIPS: Forbo; LIGHTING: Lightolier (grid, downlights); HARDWARE: Forms and Surfaces, Saino; SLIDING PARTITIONS, GLASS WALLS: Kawneer; STEEL FABRICATIONS: John DeLorenzo & Bros.; WINDOW TREATMENT: Hunter Douglas; FURNITURE: custom by Anson Woodworking, Geiger (conference table); MILLWORK: Madigan Millworks; UPHOLSTERY: Al Mercier Upholstery for G.H. Bass; APPLIANCES: Sub-Zero, Miele; FIXTURES: Franke, Speakman, American Standard.

LOCATION: New York, New York **ARCHITECT:** Parsons + Fernandez-Casteleiro PC **CONTRACTOR:** Quinn Construction Group, Inc. **SIZE:** 56,000 square feet **PHOTOGRAPHY:** Paul Warchol

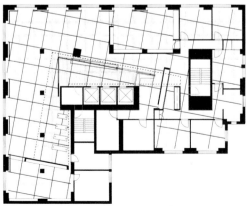

Applicazioni srl

Display & Exhibition System Producer

Across the world, nineteenth-century factories are being transformed. Their vast spaces, solid construction and ample use of wooden beams generate a multitude of possibilities from chic housing to dramatic showrooms. But when Applicazioni srl, producer of an integrated display and exhibition system named Palo Alto, approached King-Miranda Associati of Milan to retrofit an ink and sealing wax factory, little did it think that the structure would return to its original purpose as a factory. Starting off with the commission to deliver just offices, display and storage, both client and designer became convinced that the building should accommodate production as well.

Locating manufacturing on the lower floor of the two-story building, the design firm added a large cantilevered-roof lobby plus a great totem in sheet steel and brass. Leading upward is a stairway of textured aluminum with walls lined with Granital reaching an open double-height executive space directly above the lobby. This area's curved walls are lined with varnished/lacquered wood panels and bronze-covered meshing. The ceiling is the original wooden roof with beams newly cleaned by specialists. The showroom and general offices occupy the rest of the second floor and a later addition to the back of the building.

LOCATION: Dosson di Casier, Treviso, Italy
ARCHITECT: King-Miranda Associati **PROJECT TEAM:** Perry A. King, Santiago Miranda, Malcolm S. Inglis
CONTRACTOR: Cenedese-Treviso **SIZE:** 1050 square meters **PHOTOGRAPHY:** Andrea Zani

SPECIAL ELEMENTS: totem, curved wall cladding; STAIR: Falpa srl
Paderno Ponchielli (Cremona); WALL: Granital by Settef Spa; CARPET:
custom designed by Interface; LIGHTING: Sosia by Castaldi Illuminazione
(director's office), Quasar by Flos Arteluce (general office), Kriss by i Guzzini,
Spavila by Philips Lighting (exterior); FURNITURE: Pianeta Ufficio (director's office) and Zelig (general office) by Marcatré.

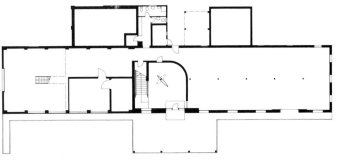

Daniel E. Snyder Architect, P.C.

....

Architecture

Aware of the need to raise client consciousness beyond conventional expectations, architect Daniel Snyder deliberately created ambiguity within his renovated office. Is the boundary between drafting space and conference area a wall, or a door? The answer is both. When open, the drafting area for three employees occupies the length of the nineteenth-century row house's ground floor. When closed to create a private space, the wall covered in gum rubber serves as a tack surface for client presentations.

Snyder employed materials to create a series of parallel zones of function within the space. One example is the conference area which changes from sheet-steel flooring and painted walls to Marmoleum covered walls, floor and ceiling. Another zone is marked by the placement of the drafting tables and the design of the library wall which can be concealed by sliding tack panels. To solve the vicissitudes of Savannah's climate a new heat pump system was installed with duct work hidden above the bookshelves and the supply plenum of the conference door/wall.

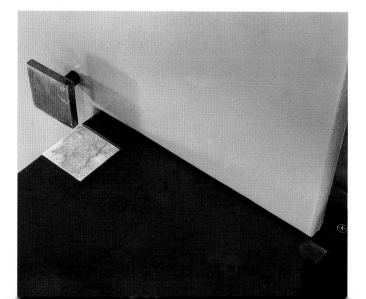

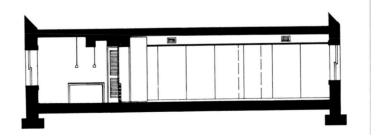

LOCATION: Savannah, Georgia **ARCHITECT:** Daniel E. Snyder, Architect, AIA **SIZE:** 956 square feet **COST:** $23,000 **EMPLOYEES:** 3 **PHOTOGRAPHY:** Tim Rhoad

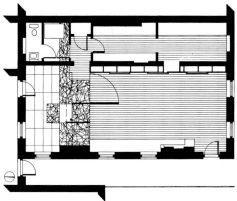

FURNITURE: Mario Botta (chair), sheet steel and Forbo Marmoleum; (custom conference table); **PAINT:** Benjamin Moore; **LIGHTING:** Leucos (pendant fixtures and drop lights), Halo (track).

MCI Communications Corporation

Communications Company

With a serious eye on safety, the design team segregated the lobby and mezzanine cluster of conference rooms from the rest of the building. Using the circular tower form as a design element on each level, STUDIOS created two executive floors with conference rooms—walls are ionized glass which give instant privacy at the flick of a switch—and dining rooms, plus nine general office floors. To keep the open offices as light as possible panel heights are limited to 48 inches and storage is concentrated in custom towers now available from the Kimball Cetra System.

Specially constructed walls and ceilings ensure ideal acoustics for the latest communications technology. The building serves primarily as a marketing venue, but MCI chose not to follow the familiar practice of presenting its wares in innovative ways by having STUDIOS design special display venues. Instead, new products are hidden from view until they are revealed to potential customers. Reinforcing the contemporary ambiance is a lively art program of American crafts, an unusual joint venture with the Smithsonian's Renwick Gallery. As the collection grows it will be given piece by piece to the American public.

Seeking to solidify its position as a major international corporation, MCI chose Pennsylvania Avenue, Washington, D.C. as its new headquarters' address. The major design challenge according to design firm STUDIOS, was to interpret corporate culture and image within the context of a speculative office building. Fortunately, the structure possessed a striking feature in the form of a vertical glass bay rising from the two-story lobby, through the intermediate floors to a dramatic back-lit glass tower above the roof.

LOCATION: Washington, D.C. **ARCHITECT:** STUDIOS, Washington, D.C. **PROJECT TEAM:** Phil Olson; Linda Wallack; Todd DeGarmo, AIA **SIZE:** 180,000 square feet **EMPLOYEES:** 250 **PHOTOGRAPHY:** Paul Warchol

COAT CLOSETS: custom designed by STUDIOS, now offered by Kimball

Cetra System; **WORKWALLS:** Geiger/Brickel; **LIGHTING:** Zumtobel.

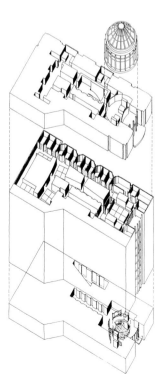

LOCATION: Los Angeles, California **INTERIOR DESIGNER:** Carmen Nordsten Igonda Design Inc. **PROJECT TEAM:** Josephine Carmen, Marco Pizzo, Harout Dedeyan **SIZE:** 9,500 square feet **PHOTOGRAPHY:** Toshi Yoshimi

Credit Lyonnais

Financial Management and Investment

O ccasionally a venerable European institution lets go of history when it reaches the West Coast. Such is the case with the financial management and investment institution Credit Lyonnais. Leaving museum quality French furniture, decorative lighting and superb art work in the New York office, the company wanted a fresh modern look with bright colored accents for California.

Carmen Nordsten Igonda Design organized a footprint with 50 percent enclosed offices sited along the perimeter wall and no traditional reception areas. On the opposite wall, interspersed with service areas, are support personnel in open plan workstations set in alcoves. This layout allows group managers to be near both their staff and departments. Entry points are signaled by a curving and widening of the interior corridor and changes in materials and ceiling height.

Cherry wood was specified for all office doors, frames and conference room furniture, and re-cut

mahogany appears in the private offices. Brilliant yellow laminate and a deep violet wool billiard cloth for acoustical wall panels provide the requested bold accents. Careful detailing unites various materials and strengthens the design. One striking example is the 14-inch square grid used as an organizing device for the several surfaces of glass, cherry wood, plastic laminate, red sandstone and fabric upholstered walls. Further examples are the custom wood storage units, conference tables and glass shelves at the open plan workstations.

FURNITURE: Herman Miller Relay, (desks, credenzas), Vecta (conference chairs, desk), ICF (lounge); **WORKSTATIONS:** custom designed to coordinate with Relay: Modo Furniture; **MILLWORK:** Artcrafters.

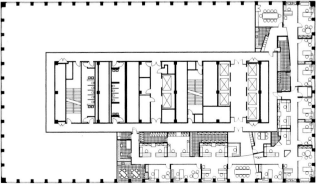

The American Trade Center

Business Center

The challenge was formidable: create a home away from home for sophisticated executives setting up businesses in Russia; offer a choice of styles ranging from high-tech to English Traditional, all executed in Western materials, finishes and furniture; and provide all the accoutrements of the modern electronic office.

Using the site of a two-year-old hotel selected by developers from Irvine, California, HCA Partners set to work importing materials, educating construction crews and educating themselves as to local codes and electrical currents. All construction products including nails and glues, furnishings and tools were specified in Los Angeles and, with the exception of some furniture shipped from Europe, sent by containership from New Jersey to St. Petersburg. HCA enlisted Italian and Finnish contractors, and arranged for American contractors—armed with detailed drawings and contract documents—to explain American construction methods and how to integrate them with Russian systems. Later workmen were sent over to detail and install paneling, carpet, wallcovering and window treatments.

After taking a wing of guest rooms and corridors down to bare walls to accommodate higher western light levels (fixtures

LOCATION: Moscow, Russia **ARCHITECT/INTERIOR DESIGNER:** HCA Partners, Inc. **PROJECT TEAM:** Gabriel C. Armendariz, AIA; Jamie Lee Roach **SQUARE FOOTAGE:** 100,000 square feet **EMPLOYEES:** 3 **PHOTOGRAPHY:** Peter Paige

were completely re-engineered and specified through Finland, Italy and the U.S. to accept 50-cycle current), HCA faced the additional hurdle of meeting city and state regulations. Wallcoverings passed a toxic smoke test by the local fire department, but only certain wool and nylon carpeting received approvals.

The new Center is a remarkable step toward a sharing of construction methods and materials.

FURNITURE: Knoll, Herman Miller, Vitra, Baker Furniture, AI, HBF;

CARPETING: Bentley, Brintons Carpet; **WALLCOVERING:** Koroseal;

LIGHTING: Lightolier, Artimide, Prudential, Leucos.

Montroy Andersen Design Group

Interior Design

Having the intention of showcasing its design and technical talents while accommodating nineteen staff members and their computer support equipment in a relatively small space, Montroy Andersen turned to classical proportioning as a design theme. The first step was to develop a three-dimensional module as a reference from which to scale each element. This was done by creating verticals in the form of tall narrow steel sculptures signifying man, horizontals in polished steel panel-wall inserts, and adding a bi-axial floor plan. Workstations, shelving and carpeting are dimensioned according to the module, including a large cabinet in the conference room which contains video electronics for presentations, and, on the side of the entrance lobby, storage and coats.

The design cognoscenti certainly appreciate such a modern steel and cherry wood interpretation of a classical approach. But, as intended, clients must marvel at the lack of obvious studio paraphernalia such as drafting tables—Montroy Andersen uses computer-aided design exclusively—and the firm's familiarity with technical

LOCATION: New York, New York **INTERIOR DESIGNER:** Montroy Andersen Design Group **PROJECT TEAM:** Vincent Cusumano **SIZE:** 2,500 square feet **COST:** $190,000 **EMPLOYEES:** 19 **PHOTOGRAPHY:** Wade Zimmerman

needs. Workstations with plastic laminate surfaces have enough space to spread out prints and hold large-scale monitors and keyboards, while full-spectrum halogen cable lights serve as task lighting. The focus of the space is the conference room where the firm presents its 3-D design and video mastery to new and prospective clients. The only enclosed area, it has a view to the rest of the office through tempered, tilted glass.

LIGHTING: Louis Paulsen (pendant), Linear (fluorescent); WORKSTA-
TIONS AND MILLWORK: Hird Blake, custom designed by Montroy
Andersen.

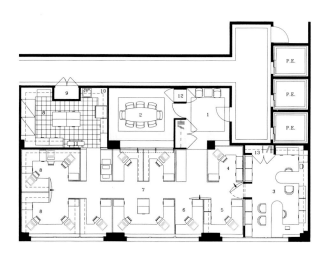

LOCATION: Nashville, Tennessee **ARCHITECT/ INTERIOR DESIGNER:** Design Collective, Incorporated **PROJECT TEAM:** Charles Smith, Eugene Daniels, Rusty Foglesong **CONTRACTOR:** Corporate Construction Manager **SIZE:** 3,850 square feet **COST:** $35/square foot **PHOTOGRAPHY:** Michael Houghton, STUDIOHIO

Design Collective Incorporated

Interior/Graphic Design, Architecture

Rarely does a design firm display its talents for the education of passersby who may eventually become clients. But when the ten-person Design Collective moved into a mixed-use complex of Historic Register buildings in downtown Nashville, it decided to create a "learning laboratory" in the atrium in full view of people on their way to offices, shops and restaurants.

With its resource library sitting in the front window, the space is an education in both finishes and materials and how a big rectangular box with a chunk taken out of one end in order to accommodate washrooms for the deli next door, can be transformed—at a cost of $35 per square foot plus $45,000 for the purchase and refurbishment of furniture—into an intriguing, colorful and spacious workplace. The firm veneered and painted the walls, used a variety of loop- and cut-pile carpeting on the floor, and left portions of the 17-foot ceiling exposed to reveal the necessities of heating, light and ventilation. A long curving beam running almost the length of the office separates the studio space from administration. Constructed from painted plywood, it is fitted with built-in downlights, suspended at heights of 7, 8, 9, 10 and 11 feet and demonstrates different ceiling heights. Another lesson is how layout and furniture can support an interactive, informal and flexible workstyle. Shared by principals and designers, the open studio space is equipped with granite tables mounted on locking wheels.

CARPET: Masland, Lotus, Helios, Richmond; LAMINATE: Nevamar; FABRIC: Herman (Eames chairs), DesignTex (library chairs); CEILING: USG; PAINT: Devoe, Zolatone; FURNITURE: Herman Miller, Knoll, Metropolitan (seating), Steelcase (table/resource library), Creative Marble (desks), Herman Miller, Planhold (pedestals, files); LIGHTING: Halo, Artimide; LIBRARY LADDER: Putnam Rolling Ladder; GLASS DOORS: Pittsburgh Plate Glass with 3M etching; MILLWORK: Middle Tennessee Millwork & Classic Executive Interiors; SIGNAGE: Columbus Sign Co.

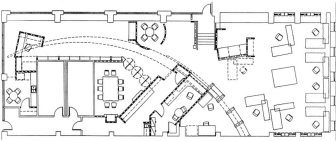

Hanna Barbera Productions

Cartoon Animation & Product Merchandising

ntegrating a dignified setting where business guests feel comfortable with the wildly energetic qualities of the cartoon art they are contemplating buying is no mean feat. Yet COE Design delivered just that for Hanna Barbera in its renovation of reception areas, conference rooms, and executive and assistant offices for fourteen employees. With a straightforward footprint, new gray painted walls deliberately slanted to echo the architecture in cartoon land, brilliant color and finishes, plus ingenious displays for products, cells and images, the new space is clearly an appropriate environment for this profitable arm of Turner Broadcasting System.

Gypsum board ceilings and walls are bright white, and in contrast, the built-in display cabinets, wall panels and window frames are finished in brilliant yellow lacquer. Custom-designed workstations glued with non-toxic adhesives have white plastic laminate desktops and orange glass transaction shelves. Television monitors continuously tuned to cartoons become live art, while Fred Flintstone and other famous heads are etched in glass. A pre-existing circular conference table, now painted white, is topped in orange glass ringed with the names of characters. The curvilinear classic furniture, too, is reminiscent of the futuristic quality of the '60s and the heyday of Hanna Barbera's prime-time success "The Jetsons."

CARPETING: Karastan Bigelow, "Northern Lights," "Newport News"; **CEILING:** Armstrong "Cirrus"; **RUBBER BASE:** Roppe; **PAINT:** Dunn Edwards; **ART DISPLAY:** custom-designed by COE Design with Arakawa art hanging system; **FABRIC:** Maharam, Tek-Wall 2000 (tack panels), Pallas, Unika Vaev (seating); **LIGHTING:** Halo, Artemide, Lithonia; **FURNITURE:** Saarinen and Bertoia from Modernica, Vitra (coffee, end tables, reception seating), Saarinen, Knoll and Jacobsen, ICF(conference seating), KI (task); **METAL FILE CABINETS:** Office Specialties/StorWall; **GLASS TOPS, DOOR, WINDOWS, AND MILLWORK:** custom designed by COE Design.

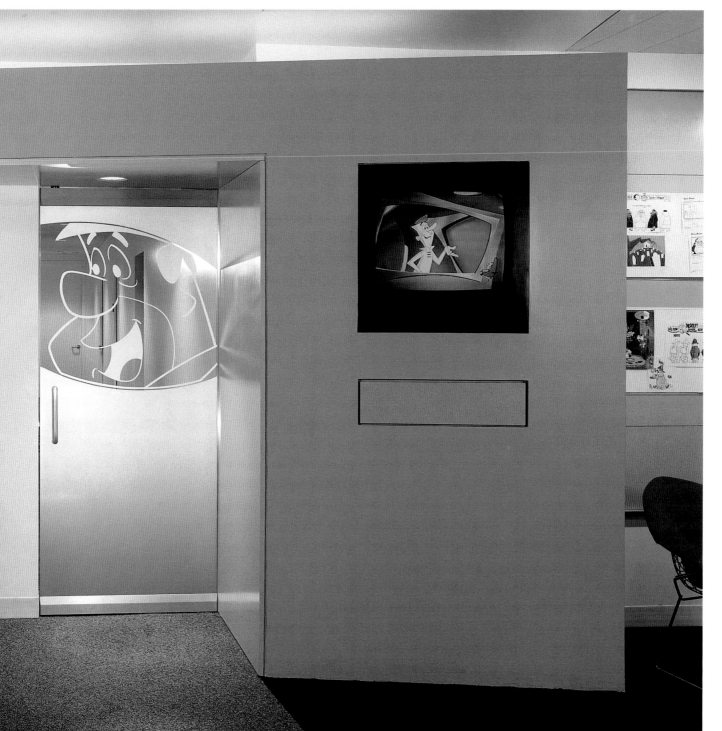

LOCATION: Los Angeles,
California **ARCHITECT:**
COE Design Architecture
PROJECT TEAM: Christo-
pher Coe, Kathryn Hamp-
ton Coe; Steven Vitalich, E.
Jon Frishman, Bill Hansell,
Hugh Lee **LIGHTING:** Joe
Kaplan Architectural Light-
ing **CONTRACTOR:** Dinwid-
die Construction Company
SIZE: 5,700 square feet
**TOTAL CONSTRUCTION
COST:** $230,000 ($40/square
foot; $41,000 furniture)
PHOTOGRAPHY: Tom Bonner

Office as Metaphor

SMALL BUSINESS OWNERS HAVE OFTEN DELIGHTED in constructing images of hot

dogs and ice cream cones announcing their culinary specialties to passersby. Today's office

metaphors are more subtle. Reflecting their business goals, the projects in this chapter

make conceptual statements concerning creativity, environment and communication.

In the business of innovative change, AXIOM's new regional headquarters is

about egalitarianism, communication and instant flexibility, while Ackerman McQueen's

entire studio expresses dramatic creativity. In contrast, the design of the Central Bank of

China is founded on the centuries-old principles of Feng Shui.

Materials are tools for articulating corporate mission and values. Employing an

ingenious mix of construction supplies and images Tsui Design and Research delivers its

mission of dynamic "living" architecture in an unforgettably whimsical form. Tsui's choice

of materials also expresses his commitment to environmentally safe workplaces.

All offices are metaphors for their business agendas. Those selected here are

among the most intriguing.

AXIOM Business Consulting

Management Consulting

AXIOM's demand for innovation as example and inspiration to clients in its new regional headquarters for a mobile work force was entirely fitting for this fast growing international management firm specializing in innovative business change. Founded on the company culture of egalitarianism and flexibility, the new sun-filled two-floor loft space is mostly composed of open plan nonterritorial offices. Conference rooms provide quiet places for large groups to meet in private, and a small elliptical room with a view to the outside offers staff an alternative spot to work quietly or make private calls.

Designed by Holey Associates, an award-winning firm noted for both aesthetic flare and mastery in solving human and technological needs, the 16-foot-high space has few permanent walls, relies on adapting furniture systems, and was built in a brief two months. A central curving wall with offices on one side offers computer hookups and temporary work surfaces on the other. The kitchen and dining space, deliberately located next to the reception area, create a spacious place for client and employee social gatherings.

LOCATION: San Francisco, California **ARCHITECT:** Holey Associates **PROJECT TEAM:** John E. Holey, Leandro Sensible, Linda Herman, Rob Wooding **SIZE:** 18,000 square feet **PHOTOGRAPHY:** Chas McGrath

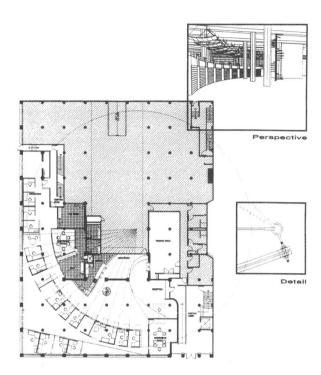

Perspective

Detail

WALL PAINT: Benjamin Moore; **STAIRCASE:** existing with distressed finish; **WALL FINISH:** custom plaster by Meiswinkel Company (kitchen and conference room).

Porter/Novelli

The words "interaction, dynamics and neighborhoods" were used by public relations firm Porter/Novelli to describe its future home. Taking these directives literally, Core delivered an environment in just twenty-four weeks which both reflects the firm's extraordinarily innovative talents and fosters interaction amongst its eighty-five people.

Innovation is expressed through the interaction of lines, planes and volumes which generate a three-dimensional layering throughout the space resulting in vistas and natural openings. This visual and tactile dynamism is reinforced with a rich mix of polished and raw materials which includes granite, terrazzo, polished plaster, glass, concrete, maple, fiberboard, and hot and cold rolled steel. A combination of direct and indirect lighting, plus fixtures illuminating vertical surfaces, adds further drama. Yet the originality of the space lies in a foot-

LOCATION Washington, D.C. **ARCHITECT:** Core **PROJECT TEAM:** Peter F. Hapstak III, AIA; Dale A. Stewart, AIA; John Abraham, RA **CONTRACTOR:** Blake Construction **SIZE:** 22,600 square feet **COST:** $48.50/square foot **EMPLOYEES:** 85 **PHOTOGRAPHY:** © Michael Moran

print intentionally designed to boost interaction. The reception area at the center of the plan contains an espresso bar, TV, and adjacent lounge where staff, consultants and clients meet informally to discuss and develop ideas. There are plenty of spaces for visible team work and doors to private offices slide open to create a 4-foot-wide opening which gives a feeling of accessibility to passersby.

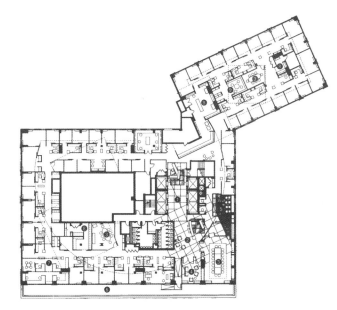

FURNITURE: custom designed by Core, Herman Miller, Corry Hiebert, Knoll, Palazzetti, ICF; LIGHTING: custom designed by Core, Coventry Lighting Associates; MILLWORK: Enterprise Woodcraft & Design.

Tsui Design and Research, Inc.

....

Architecture

A wild ecological showcase reminiscent of Yoda's cave, Eugene Tsui's architectural office provokes serious thought. Designed four years ago, it is both an adventurous place to develop and test design strategies, and an educative tool for understanding evolutionary or "living" architecture. The structural elements are continuous extensions of parts that support or are supported by the four-story warehouse, so that the building behaves like a dynamic organism rather than a static geometric box. Since comfort, safety and good health are primary concerns, all materials are nontoxic and use recycling processes.

The overall plan for the site includes an entrance with a 20-foot-high waterfall beneath an aerodynamic cantilevered "conference cocoon" in the form of an "eye," (see photograph of building model), passive heating/cooling system, and plant-based interior temperature and humidity control. Already completed, the ground floor contains the office "globe," research and conference area, kitchen, and storage located at transition areas between structural forms. Painted sky blue for expansiveness, the space is illuminated by concealed glass block in the floor. Interior walls are

LOCATION: Emeryville, California **ARCHITECT/ INTERIOR DESIGNER:** Eugene Tsui **SIZE:** 7,000 square feet **EMPLOYEES:** 5–25 **PHOTOGRAPHY:** Eugene Tsui, Amy Climo

constructed from galvanized rib-lath sprayed with recycled newspaper cellulose and water-based glue compound for acoustical and insulating purposes. Totaling some 7,000 square feet of compound curves and fluctuating arcs, the surfaces took just two days to cover.

CONSTRUCTION MATERIALS: recycled styrene, newspaper, tin cans, concrete blocks, Polygal plastic, Structolite plaster, spray-on cellulose, formed conduit and copper pipes, steel cables, trucker's rope, wood, metal, glass.

Ackerman McQueen

Advertising

clerestory windows. Banners, promotional materials and additional lighting can be hung from the unistrut ceiling grid. Reinforcing the power of the visual video message are blue floating ropes attached to pendant fixtures, a video wall of multiple images, and, at the entry, the company logo cast in light on a concrete brace. A 12-inch "line" of carpeting linking elevator lobby to conference room further signifies the power of advertising by suggesting its power to change the "lines" of communication.

onceived as a dramatic studio for creative thought, Ackerman McQueen's new quarters is literally a portrait of an advertising company whose business is the creation and communication of ideas. The site, on the twelfth floor of what once was Tulsa's tallest building, is the former drawing room of an Exxon predecessor. Stripping away seventy years of "improvements," Elliott + Associates revealed a magnificent poured-in-place structure with 14- and 18-foot ceilings, skylight openings, clerestories and structural braces.

Using light, the design firm shaped existing bold forms and surfaces, adding a multiple layering of transparency to echo the subliminal messages of advertising. The video-conferencing center, centrally located to symbolize the integration of art and business, is lit with glowing 18-foot-tall etched glass towers or by opening

FLOORCOVERING: Bentley Mills (carpeting), Kentile (hard/resilient); WALLCOVERING: Environmental Sound Control, Technique Textiles, Gillman Wale; PAINT: Sherwin Williams; CEILINGS: Sonex Acoustical; DOORS/HARDWARE: Hewi, Stanley, Corbin; GLASS: Robinson Glass, Fisher (skylight); LIGHTING Halo, Metalux, CSL, Sunnex, IPI, Peerless, National Specialty Lighting, Sure Lites, Norbert Belfor, SLD; LIGHT COLUMN FABRICATION: Robinson Glass, Buyssee Electric; SEATING: R.L. Jones, Gunlocke; TABLES: Versteel, Brueton; FURNITURE: custom fabricated by Brackel's Millwork, Spinneybeck Leather, Gunlocke (upholstery).

LOCATION: Tulsa, Oklahoma ARCHITECT/INTERIOR DESIGNER: Elliott + Associates Architects PROJECT TEAM: Rand Elliott, FAIA; Bill Yen, AIA; John Merz GRAPHICS: Elliott + Associates Architects SIZE: 17,840 square feet GENERAL CONTRACTOR: Lassiter Richey Co., Inc. LIGHTING: Phil Easion, Hunzicker Brothers PHOTOGRAPHY: Bob Shimer, Hedrich-Blessing

LOCATION: New York, New York **ARCHITECT/ INTERIOR DESIGNER:** HLW International **PROJECT TEAM:** Theodore S. Hammer; Susan L. Boyle; Peter Bachmann, AIA; Christopher Choa, AIA; Robert VerHaeghe; Ed Benovengo **SIZE:** 10,000 square feet **PHOTOGRAPHY:** Paul Warchol

Central Bank of China

International Banking

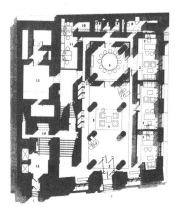

CARPETING: Prince Street Technologies; **FABRIC:** Lee-Joffa, Rodolph, Sina Pearson; **PAINT:** Benjamin Moore; **FURNITURE:** Geiger International, HBF, ICF, Bernhardt, Walter P. Sauer (custom conference table); **LIGHTING:** Linear, Baldinger, Edison Price.

erenely situated in its new home within a restored beaux arts federal registry building, the Central Bank of China of Taiwan is an exquisite example of ancient understanding influencing twentieth-century commercial design. Following the basic principles of Feng Shui, the thousands-of-years-old art of correctly arranging buildings and interiors to benefit the fortunes of their inhabitants, the bank is laid out in the form of a traditional Chinese courtyard house. The bank's entrance to the south allows the good spirits to enter (a new fritted glass vestibule "gate" guards the interior), while the conference room and adjacent chairman's office are located in the honored positions of the family hall in the center and father's room to the immediate east. Executives are placed in the sons' rooms on the east wall.

On a three-month, fast-track schedule HLW International faithfully restored the white, cream and gold-leaf finishes of what was formerly the New York State Chamber of Commerce (gold-leaf is an auspicious sym-

bol for a Chinese bank), and concealed sprinklers and building services within the beams and walls. The free-standing teak-walled conference room whose corners are butt-jointed glass and teak seats twelve around a circular table. Upholstery fabrics were selected to reiterate Chinese themes such as the chrysanthemum motif chosen for the sofas. Like many Chinese clients eager to commission Western architecture, bank executives did not request adherence to Feng Shui principles. But after this marriage of beaux arts with ancient tradition they are reportedly thrilled.

CARPETING: J & J Industries, Prince Street Technologies; VINYL: Tarkett; LAMINATE: Formica, Wilsonart; FABRIC: Maharam, Vertical Surfaces Tek-Wall (tackboard), Herman Miller (panel); VINYL BASE: Johnsonite; CEILING: Armstrong; PAINT: Duron; FURNITURE: Herman Miller.

This large progressive software company, faced with a necessary relocation in the high-tech corridor of Massachussetts, opted for a two-floor footprint which matched both the ways and nature of its work and met a strict budget of $23 per square foot. As a parallel to the Information Superhighway of cyberspace, "Avenues" and "Plazas" link and service the internal departments of the "real" office. Serving double duty as clearly marked paths for those passing through while providing convenience and privacy for the adjacent open work areas, the Avenues also contain the necessities of travel with convenient lockable storage. One area called the "Tower" provides niches to network with a laptop, answer a telephone page, or collaborate with colleagues. Another termed the "News Stand" with its topical periodicals and personal announcements serves as a social meeting place. Plazas at the intersections of Avenues coincide with breakout areas from the clustered formal conference rooms and offer open areas for dining and informal meetings.

LOCATION: Massachusetts
INTERIOR DESIGN: ADD Inc. PROJECT TEAM: Mark E. Glasser, AIA; John H. Uzee; Steven J. Basque; Eric Dumican; Deanne Bona; Karen Vagts; Karolyn Silver
SIZE: 15,000 square feet
COST: $23/square foot
EMPLOYEES: 800 PHOTOGRAPHY: Peter Vanderwarker

A Software Company

Software

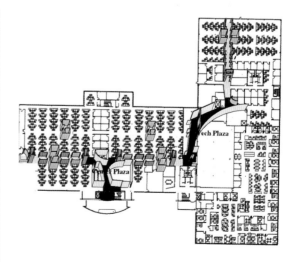

Warner International Channels

Cable

Warner wanted a lively modern space
that was appropriate to its image as both a major enter-
tainment company and player in the competitive international cable channel business. With a limited budget
for the seventy-two-person office, Carmen Nordsten
Igonda Design developed a sense of movement and play
with color, drywall shapes delineated by reveals, and a
partially skewed footprint. At the elevator lobby angled
soffits and carpet lines direct people to the reception
area where the circular ceiling and seating are arranged
as an axis point for the reception desk and video display. The circles were deliberately chosen as allusions
to the film canister and global channeling.

Following traditional custom, conference rooms
and private offices large enough for small meetings are
located on the perimeter wall. Production assistants on
the interior have modular workstations with glass partitions to allow a modicum of privacy without a closed
claustrophobic feeling. Light enters from the exterior
through opaque glass inserts in the private office doors,
and a splash of color behind each workstation softens
the corporate feeling. A newly developed curved overhead cabinet with lockable flipper doors by Knoll provides task lighting for the work counters.

FURNITURE: Knoll Magnusson Series (office); Knoll Ricchio Chairs (guest chairs), Knoll Bulldog Armchair (desk chairs); **OPEN AREA SYSTEMS:** Knoll System 6 Enhanced; **FILING AND STORAGE:** Knoll; **LIGHTING:** Lightolier (down lights), Leucos (pendants, sconces)

LOCATION: Burbank, California **INTERIOR DESIGN-ER:** Carmen Nordsten Igonda Design Inc.
DESIGN TEAM: Clara Igonda, Marco Pizzo
SIZE: 19,000 square feet
EMPLOYEES: 72 **PHOTO-GRAPHY:** Toshi Yoshimi

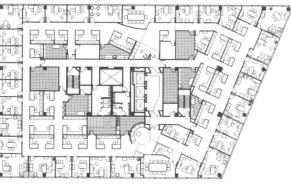

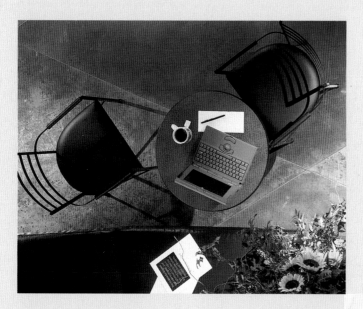

Re-Engineering Work

ALTERNATIVE OFFICING IS THE KEYWORD OF THE 90S. Innovative solutions such as ingenious flexibility for Fallon McElligott/Duffy and hoteling for Ernst & Young which is saving the firm an annual $20 million, have received the most press. But other changes that focus on workers rather than their work are equally significant.

The need for light and communication are definite musts. Informal interiors occasionally with a catered lunch as in the case of WIRED attempt to lessen the relentless stress of the high-tech workplace, while the hierarchical layout is fast becoming a thing of the past in large offices. Replacing the prestigious windowed offices that hog the daylight are universal, same-size workstations located along perimeter walls that make co-locating and teaming somewhat easier for group projects. As a further boost to communication, companies like AirTouch have installed self-service coffee bars and a choice of gathering nooks with comfortable chairs.

A revolutionary change, alternative officing is a far cry from the scientifically managed, highly controlled, often sex-segregated establishments of a hundred years ago.

has different offices for different functions. Sales people are assigned acoustically-private spaces with floor to ceiling walls. Design and editorial staff have open plan workstations with ample work surfaces, shelving and filing cabinets. Senior members chose to work at desks enclosed by 6-foot-high walls, while the circulation and advertising support staff sit in an open area bounded by 6-foot high walls which slope down in sequence so that natural light penetrates the interior. Layouts are pinned up in separate conference-type rooms for all staff to see.

Reinforcing the feeling of "home" is Cafe Wired where staff sit around a large circular table eating lunch catered by an outside service, and prepared in WIRED's kitchen. Asked to use no fluorescent lighting, Holey Associates upturned PAR 38 lamps which consume 40 percent of the state's Title 24 energy consumption allotment.

Premier publication of the online crowd, WIRED has made a big splash. Increasing subscribers geometrically and tripling staff in just 30 months after its first issue, it was time to design a new 18,000 square foot space in the old industrial warehouse of San Francisco's lively South of Market area.

President Louis Rossetto wanted to preserve the special culture of the original space and keep costs low. Also aware of the long hours put in by the very young and dedicated staff, he chose a soft-tech/office-home concept to contrast with the high-tech content of the magazine.

The footprint developed by Holey Associates

LOCATION: San Francisco, California **ARCHITECT/ INTERIOR DESIGNER:** Holey Associates **PROJECT TEAM:** John E. Holey, Carl Bridgers, Lucian Rociszewski, Mary Jo Fiorella, Ross Glazier, Sarah Wood **SIZE:** 18,000 square feet **COST:** $12/square foot **PHOTOGRAPHY:** Chas McGrath

WIRED Ventures Ltd.

....

Publishing

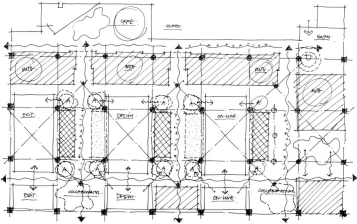

PAINT: Fuller O'Brien; **DRY WALL:** U.S. Gypsum; **FLOORING:** Armstrong, Tarkett (vinyl), Shaw, Philadelphia (carpeting); **LIGHTING:** Mulberry; **GLASS:** PPG; **SIGNAGE:** Plunkett & Kuhr

Fallon McElligott/ Duffy, Inc.

Advertising

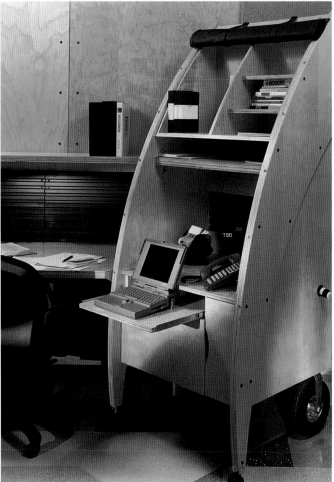

hen The Wheeler Group renovated the first of several floors into an experimental "free address" environment for hot shop ad agency Fallon McElligott/Duffy, it decided that the furniture as well as people should be mobile. Guided by agency account planner focus groups which met before and after the completion of the space, the firm created privacy and team interaction areas to be used as needed by people who spend three or four days out of the office and have no permanent or assigned desks. Work materials and personal belongings are stored in 28 roll-about unusual-shaped birch lockers equipped with an "umbilical cord" for easy power, computer and phone hook-ups. Designed with input from staff who researched proto-types, they measure 50 inches wide, 28 inches deep, 55 inches high and cost $1,200 each to build. Aware of the added advantage of conserving real estate costs, the agency will continue its re-engineering program.

LOCATION: Minneapolis, Minnesota **ARCHITECT:** James E. Young **INTERIOR DESIGNER:** Amy L. Kleppe **CONTRACTOR:** Ryan Construction **PHOTOGRAPHY:** Dana Wheelock

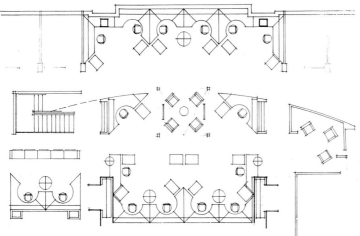

FURNITURE: The Wheeler Group, Artifex Millwork (workstations, cabinets), Steelcase "Rally" (chairs); RAIL SYSTEM: Herman Miller; LIGHTING: Leucos "Van," Halo

Apple Computer, Inc.

Research & Development

engaged in the design and, finding themselves forced to examine their own work processes, saw different ways to employ the new space as a means for organizational change.

One of four design firms chosen to develop the interiors of the buildings, Holey Associates initially met weekly with Apple project managers and users' representatives. The team developed a program and, in an

unusually constructive move to encourage participation, generated guidelines for the design process itself, coming up with goals ranging from "allow everyone to decide something" to "create a variety of different size and type of User-Defined

L istening to its engineers who appreciated openness for the exchange of ideas but stayed home to concentrate because of lack of privacy, Apple bucked its own history of open-plan offices, and chose 85 percent private offices grouped close to communal spaces for a new six-building R&D campus. Avoiding signature architecture, the company built developer-type buildings which could be easily reconfigured or sold, and boldly asked its own people to help achieve the most productive and flexible workspace possible. Ninety percent of the users

LOCATION: Cupertino, California **ARCHITECT:** Holey Associates **PROJECT TEAM:** John E. Holey, Linda A. Lawlor, Christiane C. Wendel, Leandro Sensibile, Whitney Clark, Patricia DiDomenico, Ana Gerhardt, Robert Herrera, Gabrielle Saponara. **LIGHTING:** Patricia Glascow, S. Leonard Auerbach & Associates, Inc. **CONTRACTOR:** Steve Lundberg, Rudolph and Sletten, Inc. **SIZE:** 156,400 square feet **PHOTOGRAPHY:** Chas McGrath

Area (UDA) work settings throughout the space."

The solution, unusual in its choice of circular circulation which accommodates high density, is a circle within a square configuration bounded by columns. Private offices surround two circles that are joined by labs and a double-story lobby. The UDAs are loosely linked to one another in the pie-shaped left-over spaces on the corners and windowed areas. Yellows and golds with black accents and rich terra-cottas deliver a warm backdrop for the furniture and colorful fabrics selected by employees from a menu.

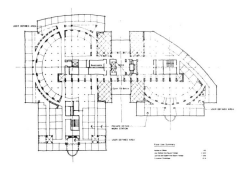

CARPETING: Bentley Carpet Mills; **VINYL:** Kentile; **LAMINATE:** Formica, Laminart, Mevamar, Pionite; **CEILING:** Armstrong; **PAINT:** Fuller O'Brien, Peirano & Peirano; **FURNITURE:** Johnson Industries (table), Bleffeplat Brayton (chairs), Martin Brattrud; **FABRIC:** Design Tex, Metaphores, Architex/Liz Jordan Hall; **LIGHTING:** Edison Price, Ron Rezeck (downlights), Staff Lighting Corporation.

Martin/Bastian Communications

Marketing

Smart designers are revamping their ways of doing business while employers are busy restructuring work styles. When architect Gary Johnson contracted to deliver what he calls a "bargain basement," efficient, fun and informal office in a turn-of-the-century industrial structure, he also agreed to a financial incentive which required designing the project for the lowest construction cost.

Searching far and wide for subcontractors who were skilled in transforming off-the-shelf items (their names, he insists, are a trade secret), he created a design that would be enhanced by the messiness of a frenetic workplace. Leftover aluminum letters from a retail project are cut into the floor to spell the name of the company; inexpensive strip fluorescents are wrapped with film negatives of quotes from clients' letters of recommendation; and a 10-foot high 250-foot long wavy sheet metal wall serves as both a divider between public tour space and private realm and a gigantic billboard of process artwork held up by magnets. On the private side with its views along two perimeter walls, employees use the same wall to post their personal memorabilia.

LOCATION: Minneapolis, Minnesota **ARCHITECT:** Gary L. Johnson, Architect **PROJECT TEAM:** Keneth Sewell, Daniel Treinen **CONTRACTOR:** Morcon Construction **SIZE:** 10,000 square feet **COST:** $275,000 **EMPLOYEES:** 35 **PHOTOGRAPHY:** Jerry Nelson

CARPETING: Karastan; **VINYL:** Armstrong; **FURNITURE:** Gary Johnson (reception coffee table), "Sistina" by Matteo Grassi (chairs); **LIGHTING:** "Delta" by Koch & Lowy (sconce).

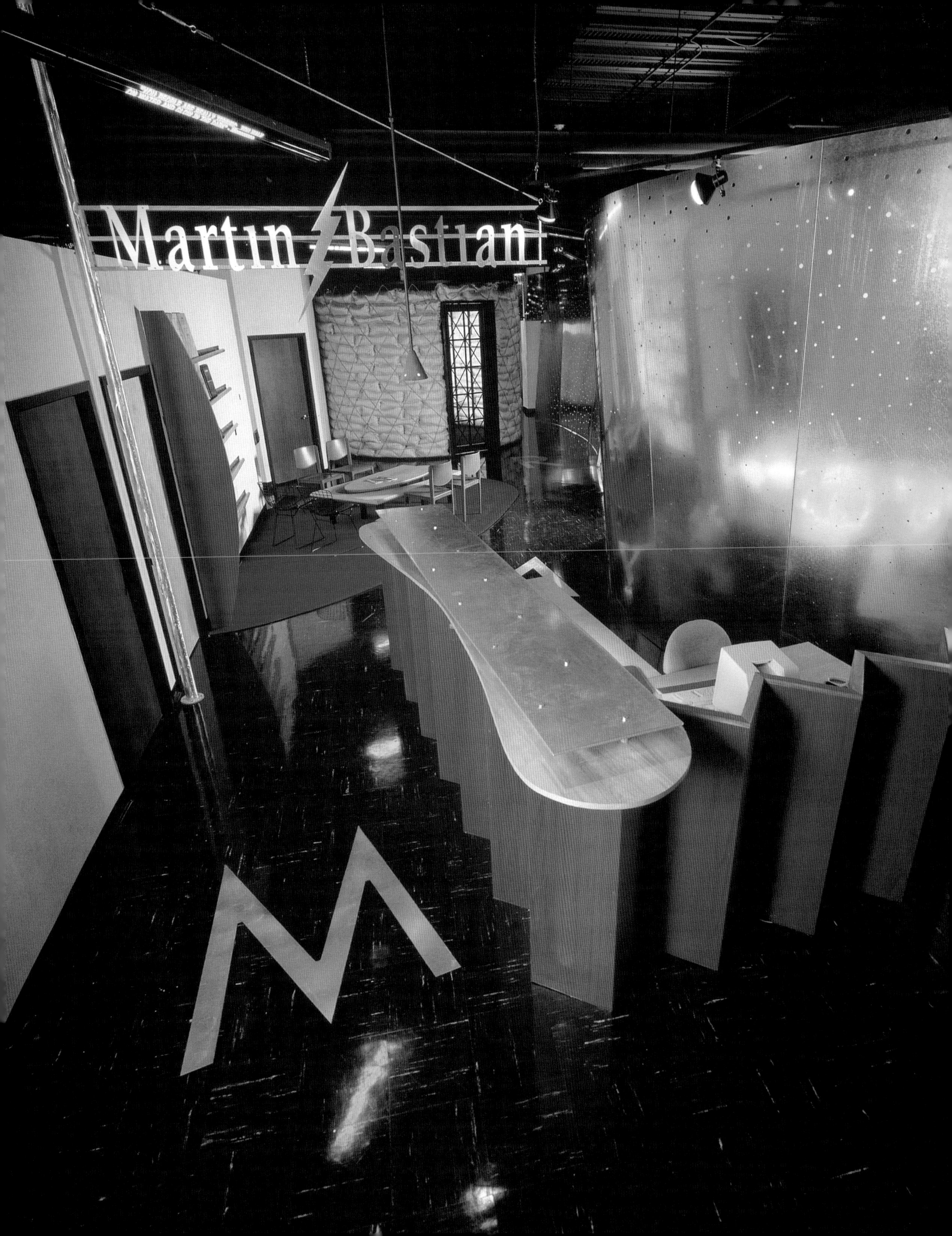
Martin Bastian

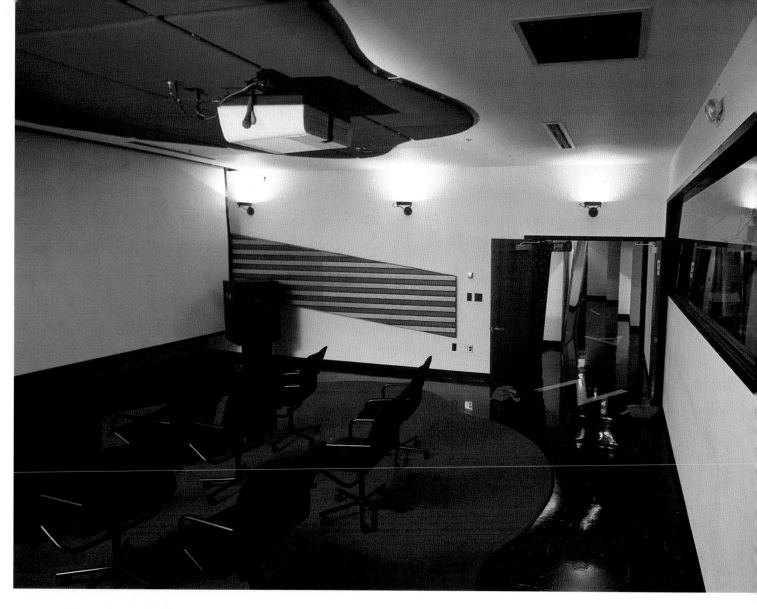

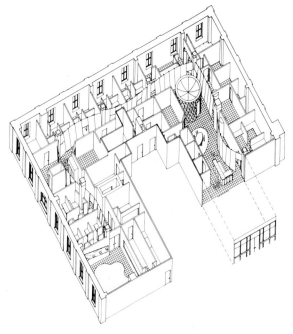

inding an appropriate identity for a one-year-old start-up corporation in the international business of wireless communications is an intriguing question. Do interactive video conferencing, real time mapping, and a headquarters wired with fiber optics for "just in time" delivery of future technology require an innovative workplace? With input from AirTouch, STUDIOS Architecture answered these questions with a warm, non-intimidating yet contemporary design fitted with spacious comfort for its occupants. An open, airy feeling with high ceilings was accomplished by raising some ceiling heights to 10-feet 6-inches—mechanical lines were fortunately located on the building perimeter. In answer to another request for an international flavor, ceilings were specified in metal, as commonly found in Europe.

Organized as an egalitarian environment with no "back of the house" feeling, views available to all and corner windows left unenclosed, each floor has gathering spaces to promote interaction amongst the 400 employees. People meet at self-service coffee bars and even the printer/copier areas are extra large so that people can comfortably talk while waiting their turn. Indirect ambient lighting softens the space, while point sources highlight the abundant artwork from countries in which AirTouch conducts business. Offices and workstations amply outfitted with fiber-optic and networking capabilities are easily reconfigurable and each workspace has its own environmental controls. STUDIOS and AirTouch jointly selected Context, Steelcase's curvilinear free-standing furniture and, with Metropolitan, developed a new individual storage/coat closet system called Template.

AirTouch Communications

Wireless Communications

LOCATION: San Francisco, California **ARCHITECT:** STUDIOS Architecture **PROJECT TEAM:** Darryl Roberson, FAIA **SIZE:** 175,000 square feet **LIGHTING:** Architecture & Light/ Darrell Hawthorne **PHOTOGRAPHY:** Richard Barnes

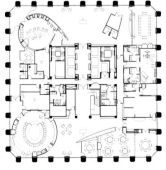

AirTouch

WORKSTATIONS: Steelcase "Context"; FURNITURE: Metropolitan

"Template"; LIGHTING: Peerless (indirect ambient).

Coregis Corporation

Insurance

which combines to form a conference table, they are large enough for small conferences. Training rooms, meeting rooms and lounges, separated in the old site, are now clustered around the reception area and can be joined together by opening pivoted doors for large gatherings.

VOA Associates established a bright new aesthetic in the reception area which resonates with both traditional and modern values. The solid round cylinder built into the wall and anigre wood doors and millwork indicate the "core" strength of the business, while a bold custom carpet and reception desk pierced with metal fins deliver a contemporary note.

rum & Forster Corporation did more than adopt Coregis as a new name and relocate to a new regional headquarters when it underwent reorganization. Dissatisfied with the hierarchical working modes traditional to the industry, the company also reinvented its image and instituted new ways of working proven by other businesses.

Universal workstations line the perimeter, letting daylight into the entire space and allowing simple "briefcase" moves when project teams change. Executive offices surrounding the building core are unusually visible with minimal frosted glass walls looking out to the open floor. Furnished with a flexible desk system

CARPETING: Lees Carpets, Flooring Resources Group, Carpets by Design; **CEILING:** Armstrong Cortega, Chicago Metallic Grid; **MILLWORK:** Herner-Geissler Woodworking Corporation, Parenti & Raffaelli Millworking (reception desk); **LIGHTING:** Pilipuf & Grist (electrical) Commerical Lighting Corp.; **GLASS:** Trainor Glass; **FURNITURE:** Brayton International (reception), Davis TAO System (private office), Hayworth RACE System (open office), Hayworth accolade (chairs); **FABRIC:** Pallas, Hayworth standards; **WALLCOVERINGS:** Knoll (wrapped panels, reception).

LOCATION: Chicago, Illinois **INTERIOR DESIGNER:** VOA Associates Incorporated **PROJECT TEAM:** Nicholas J. Luzietti, AIA, IIDA; Blair Brown, Debbie Frost **SIZE:** 97,000 square feet **PHOTOGRAPHY:** Steve Hall, Hedrich-Blessing

Anshen + Allen

Architecture

LIGHTING: Artemide, Zumtobel (suspended flourescent), Indy(non-glare accent); FURNITURE: Mies and Breur (coach hide, chrome chairs).

LOCATION: Los Angeles, California INTERIOR DESIGNER: Carmen Nordsten Igonda Design Inc. PROJECT TEAM: Josephine Carmen SIZE: 10,500 square feet EMPLOYEES: 36 PHOTOGRAPHY: Assassi Productions

In former days the fireplace and large open deck facing north toward Hollywood and the San Gabriel Mountains were the preserve of the executive elite of the old Carnation Building. Now the deck and the view—the fireplace was gutted during seismic and energy updates—are enjoyed by all the staff and guests of architectural firm Anshen + Allen.

Both client and Carmen Nordsten Igonda Design explored a variety of scenarios to determine the most democratic layout for thirty-six people which would not favor those in the older space—the original space had been doubled by the addition of an adjacent new building. Deciding that locating the reception and informal meeting areas near the deck would give everyone pleasure, the design team laid out four-person team clusters in custom workstations parallel to the southern exposure. A noncorporate atelier ambiance is supported by open ceilings with exposed mechanical and electrical services varying in height from 12 to 14 feet. In contrast, carefully detailed and acoustically controlled meeting rooms and library present a more formal setting for client gatherings.

Given an astonishingly brief four months for design and construction, all finishes other than paint were designated as "applied" features. Thus maple paneling, linen panels in the conference room, write-on boards, pin-up boards and aluminum shelving and rails were added after move in.

Johns & Gorman Films

Commercial Producer/Director

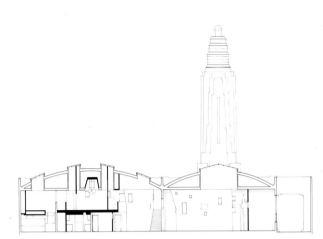

multitude of staff and free-lancers in constant need of communicating with each other. With ample natural light and private spaces for key employees, the two-level building also signals a distinct message of creative production in all its many expressions.

B ecause their workplace swells with each new production and shrinks between projects, film producers require the ultimate in flexibility. They also demand an image which speaks loudly to their creativity. Selecting a former bank building designed by D.W.L. Parkinson in the heady Hollywood days of 1928, Johns & Gorman Films turned to Schweitzer BIM to create a variety of spaces to house wardrobe, casting and client meetings, plus refreshing oases for entertaining clients.

The design response with its vertical 3-D forms clearly fits the transitory Hollywood work style with its

FURNITURE: custom designed by Schweitzer BIM, Vecta(general office seating); **LIGHTING:** Halo(downlights), Prudential(office flourescent).

LOCATION: Los Angeles, California **ARCHITECT:** Schweitzer BIM **CONTRACTOR:** Howard Construction **SIZE:** 10,000 square feet **EMPLOYEES:** 20 **PHOTOGRAPHY:** Andrew Bush

Ernst & Young LLP Great Lakes Management Consulting

Management Consulting

ne of the first corporations to research and adopt "hoteling" for its headquarters, Ernst & Young is now expanding the practice across the country. Two new identical offices in Cleveland and Dallas have multiple spaces for team conferencing and a small concierge staff which assigns workstations, posts the occupant's name outside the workspace and arranges for computer and telephone hookups. Both facilities are offspring of a lively curvilinear prototype created by Mekus Johnson in New York City, who also developed new hoteling office standards that are adapted from site to site.

For the Cleveland group, Mekus Johnson worked with users to develop two sizes of workspaces: a 162-square-foot private office (the work surface was widened and curved to hold a laptop computer) and 48-square-foot workstation for secretarial staff, short-term and, with additional storage, long-term hotelers. To solve the problem of sound in the largely open plan setting, Mekus Johnson installed white noise, lowered the

shaped acoustical tile ceilings over workstations and raised workstation panels. A reflective lighting system designed in linear patterns reduces glare and shadows.

Are employees satisfied with hoteling? Yes, says Michael Brill of the Buffalo Organization for Social and Technological Innovation (BOSTI), who conducted a post-occupancy evaluation a year after Ernst & Young first instituted the strategy in Chicago. Provided hotelers have a dedicated location for their belongings and do not receive second-class space compared with full time workers, their satisfaction increases. To the delight of the company which has considerably reduced its space costs—the Cleveland occupancy rate is 120 square feet per person—employees reported neither increase nor decrease in job satsifaction.

LOCATION: Cleveland, Ohio **ARCHITECT/ INTERIOR DESIGNER:** Mekus Johnson Inc. **CONTRACTOR:** Albert M. Higley Construction **SIZE:** 57,000 square feet **NUMBER OF EMPLOYEES:** 450 **PHOTOGRAPHY:** Jon Miller, Hedrich Blessing

FURNITURE: Knoll Morrison (workstation, private office); **STORAGE/FILING:** Meridian; **LIGHTING:** Columbia, Peerless, Duray, Kurt Versen, Lucas.

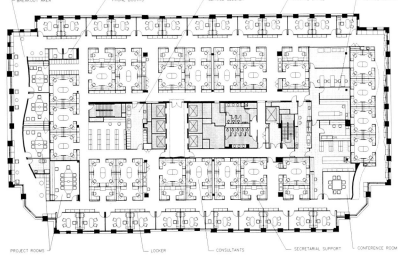

BREAKOUT AREA   PHONE BOOTHS   SERVICE CLUSTER   PRIVATE OFFICE   SERVICE CLUSTER

PROJECT ROOMS   LOCKER   CONSULTANTS   SECRETARIAL SUPPORT   CONFERENCE ROOM

Hanley-Wood, Inc.

....

Publishing

bility. Materials presented in the raw include translucent acrylic panels in gridded aluminum frames, perforated metal acoustical panels, exposed medium- density fiberboard and integrally colored plasters which take the place of wood veneers. Even the 4-foot wide rolling office doors are mounted on exposed track to reveal the mysteries of building systems.

Not content with a signature envelope, both client and design firm explored how the space could strategically impact future growth. A thorough analysis revealed the necessity for significant computer upgrades as the firm moves toward electronic publishing. At the same time it saw the need for an environment in which to test alternative organizational approaches to improve quality, productivity and creativity. So STUDIOS focused on designing offices and workstations that allow a high degree of mobility and control by the 120 staff members working alone or in teams. Offices are furnished with moveable furniture and custom wall cabinets, and workstations laid out to accommodate teams of four to six people as needed. All combine in a low-cost, highly mobile system of modular desks, mobile files and custom storage units.

LOCATION: Washington, D.C. **ARCHITECT:** STUDIOS Architecture **PROJECT TEAM:** Bruce Skiles Danzer, Jr., AIA; Jim Gerrety, AIA; John Henderson; AIA **CONTRACTOR:** Hyman Interiors **MECHANICAL/ ELECTRICAL ENGINEER:** GHT Limited **STRUCTURAL ENGINEER:** Fernandez & Associates **LIGHTING CONSULTANT:** Johnson Schwinghammer **SIZE:** 29,000 square feet **EMPLOYEES:** 120 **PHOTOGRAPHY:** Paul Warchol/STUDIOS Architecture

Design and building trade magazines face interesting choices when selecting a new home. Do they choose a bold display of identity to intrigue advertisers who deliver the bulk of their revenues, or an anonymous image reflecting corporate competence? Hanley-Wood clearly chose the former when it relocated eight magazines for the residential construction industry. Designed by STUDIOS Architecture in one and a half floors of a Class B building, the space is a direct expression of involvement with the industry and environmental awareness of endangered species and recycla-

FURNITURE: Herman Miller Newhouse modular desks, Herman Miller Relay conference tables(office, workstations), Meridian (files),millwork.

Enhancing Performance

As SOCIAL SCIENTISTS HAVE REPEATEDLY STATED, no office interior however well conceived can determine employee satisfaction, productivity or performance. Those sought-after issues are dependent upon management, its attitudes and organization, and the task at hand. But as facility managers know, design plays an essential role in supporting both investment in workspace—the mean cost per workstation in 1994 was $7,220—and performance. Colors, fabrics, furnishings and art clearly make a difference in helping people move into an open-plan environment for the first time—as employees at Coca-Cola Enterprises' new headquarters discovered.

Design supports working by establishing the partition height which encourages either privacy or communication, or by creating a sense of identity. Scrupulous design research helped deliver a functionally elegant restoration for the Bank of America in Chicago, while a spunky floor enlivens post-yuppies at fX/Morning Studios. Whatever the budget—and it can be as small as Bennett Lowry's SoHo loft retrofit— smart design clearly offers invaluable support that enhances performance in immeasurable ways.

fX/Morning Studios

....

Broadcasting

W hat better place to launch a television morning talk show than in New York with its inimitable creative edge and convenient time zone for feeds across the country? Run by the post-Yuppie generation for Rupert Murdoch's News Corporation, fX/Morning Studios is supportively playful without the relentless barrage of color, shape and texture found in the slightly older citadels of youth-oriented programming.

Given long skinny footplates of five floors with 13-foot-high ceilings in New York's Flatiron district and a budget which included significant base building renovation, HLW International established a basic back-office, administrative layout and style. The exception is the seventh floor designated as the creative level. There, bright red shelves, accent walls, and a potpourri of fabrics and furniture deliver fun, luxury and a soupçon of envy from the other floors. A curvy line of workstations for freelancers and entry level staffers extends into two offices belonging to the creative directors who can seal themselves off by closing the sliding doors. Conference rooms are deliberately enclosed in glass to avoid any feeling of claustrophobia, and walls are painted white to reflect as much natural light as possible.

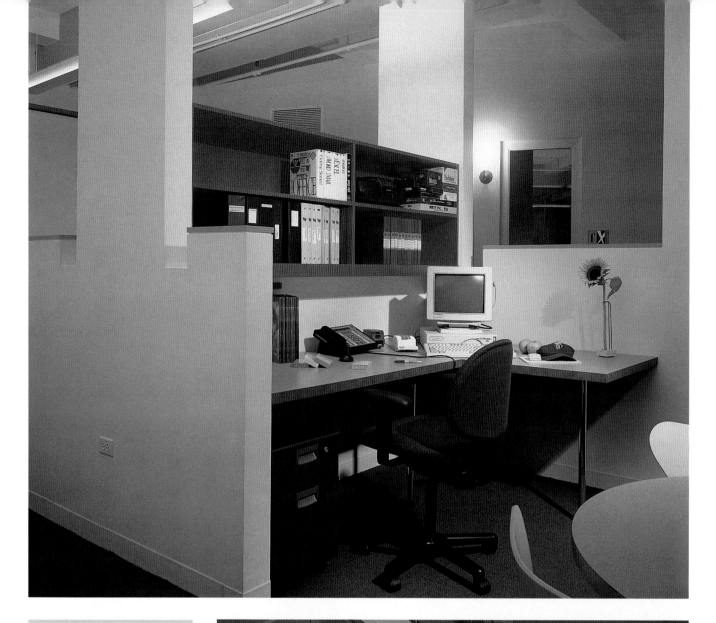

LOCATION: New York
New York **ARCHITECT/
INTERIOR DESIGNER:**
HLW International LLP
PROJECT TEAM: Theodore
S. Hammer; Susan L. Boyle;
Leslie Armstrong AIA;
Thomas Hofmann; Tim
Love; Luke Gong; Michael
Etzel; Lisa Olmstead. **CON-
TRACTOR:** Lehr Construc-
tion **SIZE:** 40,000 gross
square feet **EMPLOYEES:**
300 **PHOTOGRAPHY:** Peter
Paige

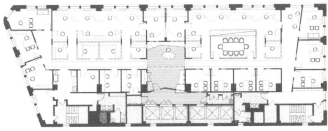

CARPETING: Pacific Crest, Prince Street Technologies; **VINYL:** Allstate, Burke; **LAMINATE:** Nevamar, Steelcase, Wilsonart; **FABRIC:** Arc Com, Donghia, Pallas, Unika Vaev; **CEILING:** Armstrong; **PAINT:** Benjamin Moore, Pratt & Lambert; **FURNITURE:** Smed, Keilhauer, Fixtures; **FILES:** Smed; **LIGHTING:** Neoray, Legion, Flos, Ron Rezek, Edison Price, Norbert Belfer.

Bennett Lowry Corporation

Architecture

Retrofitting its architectural studio loft, Bennett Lowry looked to nature and chose simple materials to stay within a $15 per square foot budget. Bright green paint, Kilim rugs and a riotous display of trees and plants add refreshing color, while warm Baltic birch and black steel were fabricated locally to supply the working, storage and meeting needs of ten employees. With the exception of office chairs, the cubicles, tables, storage, workstations, conference table, reception desk and benches are custom designed. Since the staff spends most of its days at computers, the firm designed movable low-rise workstations fitted with adjustable surfaces to comfortably fit the human body.

Choosing to maintain a sense of openess at the same time as creating a clear demarcation between public and work spaces, the firm added a touch more detail to the conference and reception area. Conscious of the dangers of environmental toxicity, steel was treated with a water-based varnish and the birch plywood rubbed with natural wax. Floors with their vestiges of former finishing are left untouched and columns painted a smart bright white.

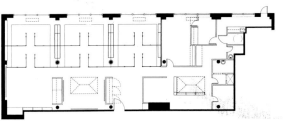

FURNITURE: Gunlocke, Jasper (office chairs), custom by Bennett Lowry

Corporation (workstation cubicles, conference table, reception desk);

PAINT: Benjamin Moore; **LIGHTING:** Luxo (task lamps).

LOCATION: New York,
New York **ARCHITECT:**
Paul Bennett Architect
EMPLOYEES: 10 **SIZE:**
3,800 square feet **COST:**
$15/square foot **PHOTOG-
RAPHY:** Wade Zimmerman

Steeped in centuries-old architecture still scrutinized and venerated by those Americans blessed with time and opportunity, Rome remains a magnificent source of inspiration. Especially interesting are firms such as 25-year-old Transit Design which represent to a greater or lesser extent, the Italian Modern Movement. Empowered through personal interaction with colleagues like James Wines, Gaetano Pesce and Frank Gehry, the principals have succeeded in interweaving the richness of the past with new possibilities.

This office for a well-know Roman advocate is one such example. Located in Rome's old city center, with medieval origins and a facade decorated in noteworthy nineteenth-century graffito, the four-story bulding presented a typical problem. How to deliver a functional modern office while complying with the tough restrictions of Italian restoration law? The architects replaced the old beams with a light transparent structure, countering it by a weightier copper element bordering the stair and elevator zone.

Reception and secretarial functions are on the ground floor. Two stories up is a waiting area for small meetings and two rooms framed with steel/glass partitions for legal assistants. More glass is featured in the lawyer's private office and large meeting room on the top floor. A delightful addition is the rooftop terrace designed for open air meetings and business lunches.

LOCATION: Rome, Italy
ARCHITECT/INTERIOR DESIGNER: Transit Design
PROJECT TEAM: Gianni Ascarelli, Maurizio Macciocchi and Danilo Parisio
PHOTOGRAPHY: Janos Grapow

Law Office

Law Firm

Bank of America

....

Financial Institution

ransforming Continental Bank's Grand Banking Hall into an efficient office for the Bank of America's private banking and personal trust departments was a formidable challenge—especially in a city known for caring about its landmark architecture.

Although the primary motive was providing 300 employees with the latest in flexible workstations and refitting historic offices as elegant and comfortable meeting spaces, a major factor was restoring the Hall to its former glory. Four hundred skilled workers from twelve disciplines over a period of ten months labored over everything from the decorative fixtures, to the 1923 Jules Guerin murals depicting international commerce that circle the central frieze. They also added amenities unheard of in earlier days such as fire and life safety systems and bathrooms for both sexes.

GHK chose large-scale trees to help humanize the monumental space with its 55-foot ceiling, designed a simple geometric circular reception desk in cherry, bronze and black granite, a low-height rectilinear granite backdrop wall, and added original Mies Brno chairs. Full height private

LOCATION: Chicago, Illinois **ARCHITECT:** GHK
PROJECT TEAM: Chris Pekarek, Howard Baskin, Rib Davis, Richard Bliss, Kathy Martin, Kim Shelbourn, Chris Nylander, Mike Lesch **CONTRACTOR:** LaSalle Construction
SIZE: 200,000 square feet
EMPLOYEES: 300
PHOTOGRAPHY: Jon Miller of Hedrich-Blessing

offices are set back unobtrusively beyond the secondary line of columns.

The design team scoured the bank's collection for antiques and reproduction pieces to furnish the newly restored conference rooms, two of which feature sixteenth-century paneling imported in 1928. It also located and returned leaded glass windows which originally belonged to the Burnham Club (named after pioneer Chicago architect Daniel Burnham). The club is now a reception room for corporate and private clients.

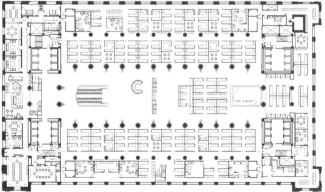

MILLWORK: Herner-Geisler Woodworking Corporation; **FURNITURE:** Knoll "Brno" (reception chairs), Spinneybeck "Derby," Calvin Textiles (upholstery), Brueton, Dunbar "Banker's Edition" (tables), Herman Miller (custom conference room table and seating); **PAINT:** Benjamin Moore; **LIGHTING:** Herman Miller Personal Light (task); **FILES AND PEDESTALS:** Meridian; **CARPETING:** Bloomsburg; **CEILINGS:** USG Interiors, Inc.

LOCATION: New York, New York **ARCHITECT:** Zivkovic Associates Architects P.C. **PROJECT TEAM:** S.D. Don Zivkovic, Brian J. Connolly, Hugh Higgins **CONTRACTOR:** LJM Construction, Inc. **SIZE:** 1,700 square feet **COST:** $36,000 (not including furniture) **EMPLOYEES:** 6 to 10 **PHOTOGRAPHY:** Ashley Ranson

to enter everywhere, while doors, canvas drapes, wood blinds, and a delightfully practical overhead glazed screen reminiscent of the surburban garage door, provide options for visual boundaries. Existing brick, oversized beams and wood joists reference the proportions of the building's massive exterior presence. In contrast with these nineteenth-century materials are predominantly white partitions, metal-framed wall systems and industrial doors. The flooring is flakeboard set within solid oak strips sealed with water-soluble polyurethane finish.

Accommodating twelve workstations, a library, storage, reception and a conference room in a limited space atop a SoHo industrial loft building is a familiar studio project for first year New York design students. But delivering a space which addresses function by ingeniously mixing custom and off-the-shelf systems product is a task for the experienced firm.

Since the six-to ten-person firm, which varies in size according to work, is organized around project teams and equality of space, a feeling of openness and visual contact was important. The solution provides that, plus a sense of privacy. The conference area is a central nucleus, surrounded by similar workstations for both principals and staff. Continuous knee-space beneath the desks also creates accessibility for people in wheelchairs.

Opaque and glazed wall assemblies allow daylight

Zivkovic Associates Architects P.C.

Architecture

CARPETING: DesignWeave, New Firestorm range, #995-Ladera, Kramer Carpet Corporation; **WOOD FLOOR:** Louisiana-Pacific chipboard; **PAINT:** Benjamin Moore; **FURNITURE:** Herman Miller "Burdick" (reception desk), custom built, painted plywood with drafting vinyl on horizontal surfaces (work desks), Sunar Hauserman (conference chairs), custom built, birds-eye maple with Avonite (conference table); **LIGHTING:** Artemide, Visa Lighting (wall sconces), Paulsen (pendants), Edison-Price (fluorescent), Lightolier (track); **CONFERENCE ROOM WALLS:** Click Systems; **CURTAINS:** sound-lined, double-faced, canvas.

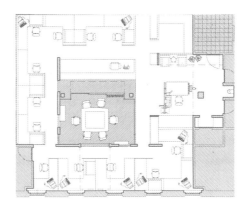

Coca-Cola Enterprises, Inc.

Soft Drink Bottler

An appropriate first corporate headquarters for the world's largest soft drink bottler, naturally features "Coke red." But Coca-Cola Enterprises wanted more than a no-frills, distinctive image for its new home occupying six floors of a second generation space with unusual floorplate. Like every other super successful company of the nineties it demanded a creative setting which would reorient employees from offices to an open work station environment, improve communications among groups, and be completed in six months—all on a restricted budget.

Having convinced the client to replace the existing rabbit warren of corridors by presenting three-dimensional images of new layouts, Stevens & Wilkinson Interiors gutted all six floors and completely redesigned each floor using a similar circulation system. Floors differ in their numbers of private offices and open plan workstations. In the general office areas there is an abundance of fabrics, finishes, textures and archival photographs of Coca-Cola's early days. Landmarks throughout the space such as a series of cubes supporting Coke bottles which project from the wall, help employees and visitors find their way.

The four top executives

LOCATION: Marietta, Georgia INTERIOR DESIGNER: Stevens & Wilkinson Interiors, Inc. SIZE: 120,000 square feet PHOTOGRAPHY: Marco Lorenzetti, Korab, Hedrich-Blessing

believe it an overwhelming success and employees granted their highest accolade after occupying it for a year, by not voicing a single complaint.

FURNITURE: Steelcase (office workwall, table and desk, workstations, task and side chairs, receptionist chairs), Vecta (side and work chairs, conference table and chairs), Metro (lounge chairs), Brayton (end tables, reception sofa), Prazmatique (reception coffee table), Knoll (reception end table), Signature (custom reception desk); **MILLWORK:** Healy Roddy Chrisler; **CEILING SCREENS:** Andree Studios.

Swid Powell

Design

To streamline business, Swid Powell, a design team which has developed an interesting niche commissioning tabletop products from architects and designers, decided to consolidate its warehousing and administration by moving into a loft space. Instituting a "just-in-time" system where products would flow from manufacturers to retailers without lengthy stays in inventory, the firm also needed close and informal interaction amongst its twenty people.

The solution of a "big room" bounded by fixed and moveable screens proved to be the answer. Architect Paul Gates developed an elegant system of steel columns, thin partitions and sliding translucent laminated glass panels to frame the central open workroom, and provide a sense of privacy for the enclosed offices.

The existing interior was whitewashed, huge pivoting windows were refurbished and maple and concrete floors sanded and finished. The two types of column—one from the turn-of-the-century construction and the other from a '20s addition—were scraped and left as contrast between old and new. To avoid a tangle of wires leading from the perimeter walls, cabling was run in the cavity beneath the flooring to allow desks to be placed in the center of the space.

LOCATION: New York, New York **ARCHITECT:** Paul Gates Architect **INTERIOR DESIGNER:** Stephen Sills & Associates **PROJECT TEAM:** Paul Gates, Architect; Stephen Sills, James Huniford **SIZE:** 10,000 square feet **EMPLOYEES:** 20 **PHOTOGRAPHY:** Paul Gates

Serving also as a showroom, the entry has bent steel plates as display shelving. Steel was also used in the large simple tables designed to create an open feeling and encourage communication.

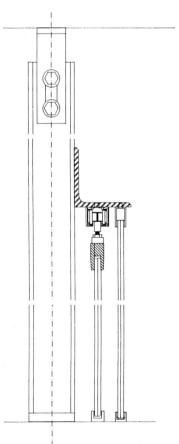

PAINT: Benjamin Moore, Pratt & Lambert; **FURNITURE:** custom designed by Paul Gates Architect, fabricated by Robert Isabell (desks); **LIGHTING:** custom light fixtures by Paul Gates Architect and Fisher Marantz Renfro Stone.

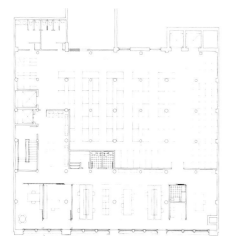

United Media

....

Licensing and Syndicating

A beautifully balanced design that stretches talents and delivers function, the new United Media HQ is the result of that rare combination of imaginative and determined client, and responsive firm experienced in media design.

Working closely with the young expanding subsidiary of Scripps Howard, whose business is licensing and syndicating accounts such as Peanuts, Home & Garden Television (HGTV) and National Geographic, HLW International listened to demands for a professional, businesslike and creative image that was neither a crazy ad agency nor a bank. The first decision was to create some dynamism in the 45,000 square foot floor plate by designing a massive diagonal "zone." Slicing from north to south with open ceilings and dramatic lighting, it includes the reception area with its burnished steel desk, a lockable raw-steel-and-glass-enclosed 980-square-foot showroom of licensed goodies for sale, and an abundance of formal and informal gathering places. The entrance to the conference room is through three asymmetrical pivoting doors paneled in oversized illustrations, which can be left open for receptions.

The quieter work areas are finished in white and gray tones with accent colors from the zone's subdued palette of cherrywood, dark blue, red, gray and ocher. Translucent doors and comic characters etched on glass sconces lighten the office hallways, and artwork and cartoons featuring United Media's characters are spread through the floor.

Happy to be closer together in a smaller space, the company has grown exponentially since moving in. Two small conference rooms are added to the southern end of the zone and the open comfy lounge spaces have been replaced by workstations.

LOCATION: New York,
New York **ARCHITECT/**
INTERIOR DESIGNER:
HLW International L L P
PROJECT TEAM: Leslie
Armstrong, Susan Boyle,
Joseph Calabrese, Dominic
Cardinale, James Conti,
Steven Darr, Michael Etzel,
Lorelei Guttman, Thomas
Hofmann, Gail Ressler
CONTRACTOR: Lehr Con-
struction **SIZE:** 45,000
square feet **PHOTOGRA-**
PHY: Peter Paige

CARPETING: Interface, VINYL: Estrie, Tarkett, LAMINATE: Formica,
Nevamar, Wilsonart; FABRIC: Knoll; CEILING: Armstrong, Hoyt, Pratt
& Lambert; PAINT: Benjamin Moore, Pratt & Lambert; WOOD WALL
FINISH: Patella; FURNITURE: Knoll, Herman Miller; FILES: Meridian;
LIGHTING: Neoray, Lightolier, Louis Poulsen, Visa Lighting, Zumtobel.

The Morris General Agency

Insurance

n true Frontier spirit the Morris Agency ignored the current notion of the ideal workplace where identical workstations, open spaces for open communication, and places for getting together in teams are *de riguer*. Instead, the new building by Elliott + Associates is organized according to function and hierarchy, with the "better" offices reserved for those insurance folk who have put in time and earned their dues.

Inspired by the wind, respected by Native Americans as a mysterious force visible only as it moves through the tall prairie grasses, the building responds to the elements in its 2-acre setting. The protective north side has small windows; the west is closed against the harsh sun; the

LOCATION: Oklahoma City, Oklahoma **ARCHITECT/INTERIOR DESIGNER:** Elliott + Associates, Architects **GENERAL CONTRACTOR:** Smith & Pickel Construction Co. **ENGINEERING:** Bill Boyd (structural) **LIGHTING:** Phil Easion, Hunzicker Brothers **SIZE:** 8,700 square feet **PHOTOGRAPHY:** Bob Shimer, Hedrich-Blessing

eastern facade features a "sunrise" window at the spine intersection. New sales people are assigned the "remote" two-person offices, while the successful veterans enjoy a light-filled southern exposure through 10-foot-wide by 12-foot-high windows overlooking a 3-acre lake. Linking all spaces in the long narrow structure, the skylit center spine serves as an art gallery with glimpses of the prairie grass seen through 10-inch-wide and 1-foot-tall "walking windows."

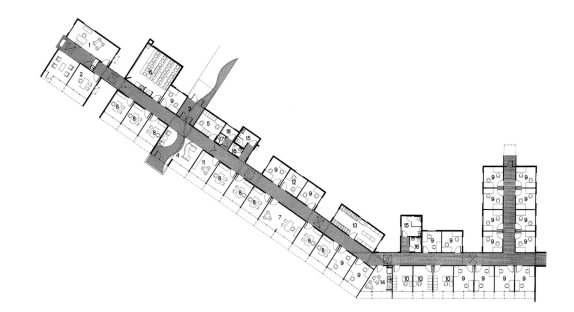

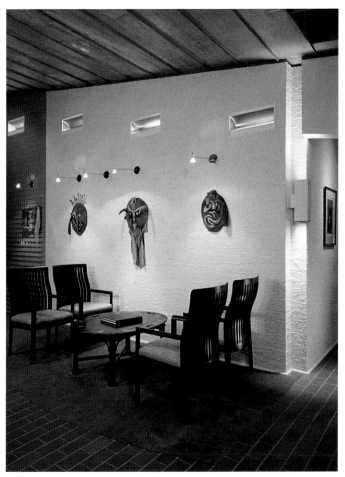

FLOORCOVERING: Mannington Harcourt — Bentley Mills Dunhill (carpet); Kentile (hard/resilient); Endicott, American Olean (brick tile); **WALLCOVERING:** I.D.S., India cotton; **PAINT:** Sherwin Williams; **CEILINGS:** Armstrong Second Look III; **DOORS/HARDWARE:** Hager, Yale, Schlage (copper clad door), Southwestern Roofing of Oklahoma City (fabrication); **WINDOWS/GLASS:** Pella, Amarlite, Pella Pecot (skylight); **SIGNAGE:** Elliott + Associates, Architects (design), Southwestern Roofing, J & B Graphics (fabrication); **LIGHTING:** Halo, Engineered Lighting Products, Metalux, Beghelli, Fine Lite, Lumark, Alkco, Norbert Belfer, Flos, Louis Poulsen, CSL.

Image as Message

"RESTRAINED," "NOTHING TO HIDE," "COST CONSCIOUS," and "non-hier-

archical" characterize the new office. Materials tend to be light and natural and the

furniture contemporary rather than conservative. Extravagances of scale found a

decade ago in top management suites are rare exceptions as more executives opt

for egalitarian quarters, sometimes sitting in the same-sized cubicle as their secre-

taries. Even the oversized executive chair, that traditional symbol of power, has

shrunk as more women move into management positions.

Yet the office of the '90s has not forgotten its core purpose to present

itself as stable, financially responsible and worthy of trust. So the new image also

reflects a functional correctness that bows to the need for both substance and

stringency. The National Minority AIDS Council and Blackrock Financial

Management, both intentional responses to the expectations of their clients, are

prime examples. The former uses off-the-shelf materials while the latter bypassed

custom furniture for its boardroom—yet both express images of power and stability.

Putnam Investments

Investment/ Financial Management Firm

After expanding its business from private money management to working with clients in the institutional and pension business, Putnam CEO Lawrence Lasser asserted, "We need an image, something that says 'Putnam' when clients walk through our door." Putnam also wanted a flexible space which could quickly respond to the vagaries of the market; reduce employee square footage to help increase headquarters capacity by one fourth; and encourage communication among its 924 employees. The renovation program for nine existing plus three additional floors included a new open plan to private office ratio of two to one, four private dining rooms, a conferencing center with six individually styled rooms fitted with state of the art communications, and high-tech trading areas.

Elkus/Manfredi Architects transformed the existing mahogany conservative look by lightening and softening materials—white-washed oak, stainless steel, floor-to-ceiling fritted glass, and curved walls; adding abundant natural light through clerestories and specifying *la creme* in classic contemporary furniture. When visitors step onto the reception floor they enter a vestibule with blue padded leather walls and a sculpted wave in the ceiling whose motif is subtly echoed throughout the space on door handles, tabletops, and the new stairway. The art collection selected by a consultant ranges from Lichtenstein to a host of promising local unknowns.

WALLCOVERING: Carnegie, Fairmount Fabrics, Liz Jordan Hill for Architex, Manuel Canovas Inc., Willow Tex Inc.; **PAINT:** Benjamin Moore, Polomyx, Martin Senour; **LAMINATE:** Laminart, Nevamar; **MASONRY:** Berkshire Constructions Services; **FURNITURE:** Atelier International, C.I. Design, Herman Miller, ICF, Knoll, Matteo Grassi, Vitra (seating), Acerbis International, Atelier International, Colonial Marble, Davis Furniture Systems, Estel Inc., Flexform, Knoll, Charles McMurray, Sographos (tables), Office Environments (vendor), custom manufactured by Wall/Goldfinger Inc., DatesWeiser, Charles McMurray Design, DeÇlercq International; **FLOORING:** Forbo; **CARPETING:** Bentley Mills, V'Soske; **CEILING:** Armstrong; **DOOR HARDWARE:** Almet; **GLASS:** Salem Glass; **RAILINGS:** American Arc and Plymouth Rail; **UPHOLSTERY:** Spinneybeck, Bernhardt; **ARCHITECTURAL WOODWORK:** Walter A. Furman, Inc., A.H. Leeming; **CABINETS:** Walter A. Furman Inc., A.H. Leeming, Wall/Goldfinger, Dates Weiser; **PLANTS/PLANTERS:** Earthenware of Thailand; **LIGHTING:** Cedric Hartman, Joseph Lehr, Andree Putnam for Baldinger.

LOCATION: Boston, Massachusetts **ARCHITECT:** Elkus/Manfredi Architects Ltd. **PROJECT TEAM:** Howard F. Elkus FAIA, RIBA; Elizabeth Lowrey Clapp; Lee M. Pearce; Alison Gillies; Scott Allen; William J. Barry, AIA; Douglas Cheung; Sheila Craig; Edward Fischer; Rena Gyftopoulos; Sara Harper; Kristen Kennard; Robin Komita; Sara Lopergolo; James Macdonald; Jennifer Maiorani; Gary Marotta; Suzanne Molloy; Rennell More; Kelton Painchaud; Toby Sirois; Sumio Suzuki; Laura Ulvestad **CONTRACTOR:** Beacon Construction Company **LIGHTING DESIGNER:** Fisher Marantz Renfro Stone **GRAPHIC DESIGN:** Carbone Smolan Associates **SIGNAGE:** Green Dot Design **SIZE:** 210,000 square feet **EMPLOYEES:** 924 **PHOTOGRAPHY:** Marco Lorenzetti, Korab/Hedrich-Blessing

Blackrock Financial Management

Asset Management

n the heydays of the eighties, designers toured Europe buying antiques and selecting marble for ever-larger financial kingdoms. Now when a financial firm orders new accommodations, the first and foremost request is that they be "cost conscious." Such was the case with Blackrock Financial Management, a start-up asset management firm which split off from The Blackstone Group. The new company wanted an image that was separate from Blackstone, elegant, contemporary in feeling, and featuring natural materials.

Before beginning its design Mancini Duffy cut construction costs by retaining portions of the existing fit-out of the newly leased space which later were designated as perimeter private offices. By adding a frosted glass sidelight lacquered to deliver a hand-crafted appearance, carefully detailed natural cherry doors, frames, flush base and crown molding, and top-of-the-line flexible systems furniture, the offices achieved an appropriately professional look.

Rather than go to the expense of custom designed furniture for the boardroom, the firm specified chairs designed by Mario Bellini, and credenzas and table finished in cherry veneer from the Geiger International Triuna collection. A six-foot-wide broadloom carpeting with integral cushion back extends throughout the office with the exception of the raised 40-person trading floor which is covered in carpet tile.

Hand-made sand-textured wallcovering, cherry base and crown-molding, and a honed-finish French limestone border were selected for the reception area which is often used for assembling before special parties in the boardroom. The stepped cherry-framed glass wall separating the reception area from the boardroom is crafted in double layers of carved glass to provide interest and translucency. Stored in the credenzas are linens, a complete service for 40 in Limoges Celadonware, Chistofle stainless flatware, and crystal stemware. The wine cellar is built into the pantry area.

CARPETING: Interface; **VINYL WALLCOVERING:** Carnegie fauxsilk fabric; **LAMINATE:** Formica; **CEILING:** Silhouette Armstrong Cirrus tile, Decoustics Panel Fabric System G; **PAINT:** Benjamin Moore; **FURNITURE:** Geiger Petri Systems (desk and workstations), Contour (private office seating), Geiger Triuna (conference room table, credenza and reception desk), Vitra Figura (conference room seating), Geiger International (secretarial workstations), Donghia (reception seating), Geiger/Brickell (guest seating), SBFI; **GLASS PARTITION:** The Degnan-Laurie Glass Studio; **RAISED TRADING ROOM FLOORING:** Tec-Crete Cornerloc; **LIGHTING:** Linear, Lightolier, Kurtversen.

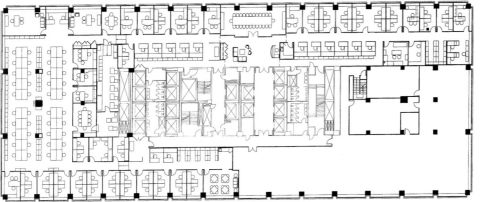

LOCATION: New York, New York **ARCHITECT/ INTERIOR DESIGNER:** Mancini Duffy **PROJECT TEAM:** Ralph Mancini, Jeffrey Tobin, Carolyn Brooks **CONTRACTOR:** StructureTone **SIZE:** 25,000 square feet **PHOTOGRA- PHY:** Paul Warchol

ESEO Federal Credit Union

Credit Union

t was an interesting exercise when ESEO board members and staff sat down in separate brainstorming sessions to create a portrait of themselves. The board used the words family atmosphere, membership-owned, frugal and trustworthy. The staff saw themselves as family oriented with an average age of 35 to 40, working class, and hourly wagers with a focus on enjoying life. So when Elliott + Associates developed a master plan for the new site which allowed for additions and an orchard of 53 redbud trees to commemorate the age of the institution (the redbud is Oklahoma's state tree), it also created a building which embodied both the personality and goals of the company and an open atmosphere. Programming requirements included loan service offices, a vault, conference/board room, shared stations for lobby and drive-in tellers, and support functions.

Like the leafy canopy of a tree supported by a thick trunk, the roof with its steel columns shelters the credit union from the cold north winds and piercing summer suns. Indigenous materials of stone, wood, rusting steel, and aggregate floors communicate frugal

LOCATION: Oklahoma City, Oklahoma **ARCHITECT/INTERIOR DESIGNER:** Rand Elliot, FAIA; David Foltz; AIA **CONTRACTOR:** Smith & Pickel Construction **LIGHTING:** Phillip Easion **SIZE:** 7,800 square feet **PHOTOGRAPHY:** Bob Shimer, Hedrich-Blessing

unpretentiousness, while the soaring roof evokes the feeling of working out of doors under the shade of a great tree. In recognition of a Native American presence is the giant circle of stones outdoors and four sacred colors—red, yellow, black and white—painted on the conference storage cabinet.

FLOORCOVERING: Prince Street Technologies, Kentile (hard/reslient); **PAINT:** Sherwin Williams; **CEILINGS:** Tectom Panels, T111 plywood; **HARDWARE:** Schlage; **GLASS:** Knox Glass; **SEATING:** Kron; **FURNITURE:** Imel Woodworks (custom fabricator); **LIGHTING:** Norbert Belfer, Indalux, Lumark, Kenroy Trolli; Metalux, Alkco, Hubbell, Halo, Lightolier, Artemide.

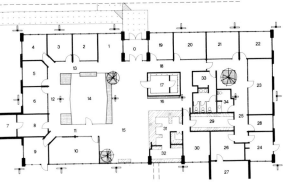

Baker & McKenzie

Law Firm

Being an international law firm, Baker & McKenzie wanted an international look that was not too flashy or regional. It also wished to communicate comfortable success without being ostentatious or overly lavish. Moreover, the 475-person firm required a design which met the expectations of its various practice groups, each of which demanded considerable say in the final design direction.

Design firm Mekus Johnson listened to all and responded to the many points of view by creating a "common ground" articulated in a contemporary, timeless, international theme. Employing minimal ornamentation, layered ceiling surfaces, clerestory glass, and broad vertical surfaces of traditional stone, marble, and dark-toned woods, the design team delivered a clean, energetic style that is mildly conservative. The hundred-plus attorneys were satisfied and also appreciated the functional organization which allows for future expansion.

The footprint is efficiently organized by having secretarial support staff and casework filing located directly across a main corridor from attorneys' private offices. To meet the technological demands of

LOCATION: Chicago, Illinois
ARCHITECT/INTERIOR DESIGNER: Mekus Johnson Inc. SIZE: 238,000 square feet EMPLOYEES: 475
PHOTOGRAPHY: Jon Miller, Hedrich-Blessing

small and large groups, the team designed a sophisticated 23,000-square-foot "Inns Room." Equipped with built-in, concealed monitors, A/V system, and adaptable for any sized gathering, the space serves both communication and dining needs.

WORKSTATIONS: Stow Davis (private office); FURNITURE: Kron Manolete (reception seating), Steelcase Sensor (task seating); UPHOLSTERY: Parenti & Rafaelli, Edelman leather (custom reception sofa), Carnegie Tosca (secretarial seating); FILES/CABINETS: Office Concepts; LIGHTING: Kurt Versen, Edison Price, Peerless (reception area), Zumtobel (private office).

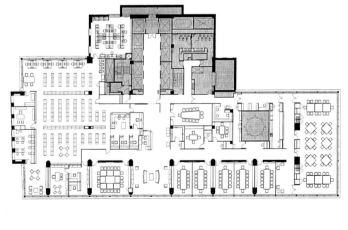

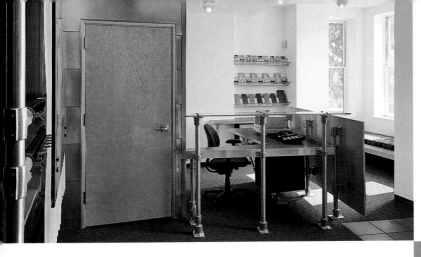

onstructed from two derelict row houses destroyed in the 1968 race riots, the award winning headquarters of the National Minority AIDS Council was deliberately designed to send powerful messages: future prosperity for the neighborhood; remember all who have died of AIDS; and hope for those presently ill. Many parts of the exterior and interior were kept intact to represent the stability of the organization, now the axis of all HIV/AIDS focused community-based organizations. But the new interior is organized around group interaction expressing the belief that through the cooperation of many, help will be found for the ill.

Crafted by Core from a dramatic mix of old exposed red brick, original beams, and glass and metal pipe, the space is tightly organized to provide a transparent working space for 44 people. Most workstations are in shared spaces, with private offices located on the front and back walls. A sliding wall dividing the conference and lunch rooms can be moved to provide a large meeting space. To meet the tight construction budget of $93 per square foot, most of the lighting was custom designed, and furniture and work stations constructed from off the shelf particle board, melamine, and perforated metal.

LOCATION: Washington, D.C. **ARCHITECT/INTERIOR DESIGNER:** Core **PROJECT TEAM:** Peter Hapstak III, AIA; Dale A. Stewart, AIA; Vyt Gureckas, AIA; Sean Wayne **CONTRACTOR:** Malin Construction **SIZE:** 7,500 square feet **PHOTOGRAPHY:** © Michael Moran

National Minority AIDS Council

Non-Profit Association

Arnall, Golden & Gregory

Law firm

The partners of Arnall, Golden & Gregory wanted a "light and airy" feeling for their new offices. Eager to break with the dark and somber tone of the stereotypical lawyers' office, they also required a footprint that efficiently and functionally helped communication between partners, staff, and services which is often lost when attorneys are spread over several floors.

Faced with a short six month construction schedule due to leasing delays, Stevens & Wilkinson Interiors requested early approvals on long lead items such as

structural steel, marble flooring and custom fabricated handrails for the monumental stair which links four floors. To guide visitors from the elevator lobby to the reception, conference and dining areas, the design team created an angled wall faced in gridded anigre panels. In another move to take advantage of the firm's location on the 26th through 29th floors, it sited the stair on the perimeter of the building so all could enjoy the stunning views of downtown Atlanta. The floor plan includes partners' offices and their support staff on each working floor.

The attorneys requested that the large conference rooms be sized to allow 6 feet of circulation room around the tables, and that there be additional small "war rooms" close to their offices—these were sited at every corner. Behind each cluster of secretarial stations are work areas for sorting and processing papers and housing copiers and fax machines. To diminish screen glare, stations are equipped with task lights and low light-level, compact fluorescent downlights. Halogen track lighting on dimmer switches highlight the firm's extensive photography collection.

FURNITURE: Johnson Industries (dining tables), Bernhardt (dining and conference chairs, reception lounge seating), Knoll (workstation chair), American Studio Group (custom reception tables), Peter Alexander (reception side chairs), Denton Bragg (custom credenza in partner's office), Charles McMurray (partner's office seating); **WALLCOVERING:** Maya Romanoff (partner's office); **CARPETING:** Harbinger (dining), Karestan-Bigelow (partner's office, conference room), Edward Fields (reception); **RECEPTION ARTWORK:** Frank Stella from AG&G collection; **MILLWORK:** Patella Woodworking.

LOCATION: Atlanta, Georgia **INTERIOR DESIGNER:** Stevens & Wilkinson Interiors, Inc. **SIZE:** 82,000 square feet **PHOTOGRAPHY:** Marco Lorenzetti, Korab/Hedrich-Blessing

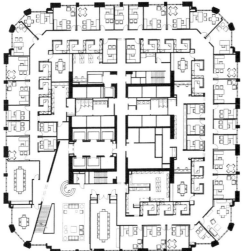

The Timberland Company, Inc.

Footwear Manufacturer

ocated in a renovated building deep in the woods, organized around a footpath which leads through fields of green-carpeted open office, this footwear manufacturer's image is synonymous with the outdoors. To encourage interaction and communication, the design firm ADD Inc. sited public spaces along the edge of the meandering interior trail. Among them are team workstations, shared conference rooms, coffee stations, and boldly shaped copy/fax areas.

As further support to the rural image, ADD devised a nature-inspired palette for the fifteen-year-old, two-story office and light manufacturing building. Natural maple, cherry wood, stone, rusted metal and natural steel and copper add to the casual persona, while the glass-walled conference rooms are finished in the colors of the seasons. Four new interconnecting skylit stairs, each bordered on one side by a double-story wall serving as a display space, present more opportunities for the 600 employees to catch up on company news.

LOCATION: Stratham, New Hampshire **PROJECT TEAM:** ADD Inc. **SIZE:** 190,000 square feet **PHOTOGRAPHY:** Richard Mandelkorn

CARPETING: J & J Industries (general office), Carpet Systems (trail and stairs), Millliken (lobby), Larsen (lobby area); **STONE:** Indian slate tile; **LEATHER PANELS:** Brayton; **PAINT:** Benjamin Moore; **OFFICE SEATING, FILES AND SYSTEMS:** Steelcase; **OCCASIONAL CHAIR AND LOBBY SOFA:** Metro; **MILLWORK:** The Woodworks; **MEETING TABLE:** Herman Miller; **LIGHTING:** Halo and SPI.

worth Magazine

Publishing

For its new publication *worth*, Boston-based Fidelity Investments, Inc. demanded a space which "speaks to the New York vernacular," while maintaining a combined buildout and furniture budget of $55 per square foot. To meet the six-month occupancy schedule, the firm's Facility Design & Construction Division, which had already developed preliminary space layouts and design concepts, teamed up with GHK. Working together they streamlined the decision-making process and eliminated sign-off delays.

Seeking architectural inspiration, the design team turned to the Chrysler Building, a New York icon which happened to be part of the view from the new *worth* offices on Lexington Avenue. Studying the top of the building's bold angles which soften and radiate to a curve, the team lopped off corners of rooms and angled corridors to encourage communication. To avoid a cluttered workspace, GHK designed slanted shelves covered in blue fabric as a place to store and display graphics in progress.

Responding to further instructions from the client that the space "promote a slick yet restrained image, and look smart, bold and substantial," it borrowed from Fidelity's Mondrian and Miro painting collection for color palette and finishes. Red, yellow and blue of the Rietveld chair from the same period as the Chrysler Building, are repeated in the reception desk.

WORKSTATIONS: Herman Miller "Ethospace"; **CARPETING:** Harbinger, Custom Black "Confetti"; **VINYL:** Armstrong; **FABRIC:** Herman Miller; **FURNITURE:** Herman Miller "Equa" (workstation/private office seating), Knoll "Newhouse" (reception seating); **LIGHTING:** Zumtobel.

Tainer Associates, Ltd.

Architecture and Graphic Design

As many firms have discovered, a loft space is a giant three-dimensional blank slate waiting to express the persona of its occupants. Given a building's framework of several thousand square feet, designers have enjoyed either superimposing their mark to the exclusion of existing architecture, or integrating contemporary themes with features from the past. Tainer Associates chose the latter.

Employing the ceiling grid as a module, the space is organized into public and private realms. The public areas have lowered ceilings to encourage a more intimate feeling, while the workstations along the window wall are left open to the exposed utilities. Reinforcing the separation is a 65-foot interior gallery with an open portico-type wall topped by a grid on one side. In contrast, the other wall is plastered, gouged, and painted to show wear, tear, and a depth which conjures images of old Europe. Used for pinups (the distressed finish disguises marks and pinholes), the wall is painted in contemporary colors to emphasize the juxtaposition of old and new.

LOCATION: Chicago, Illinois **ARCHITECT/INTERIOR DESIGNER:** Tainer Associates, Ltd. **PROJECT TEAM:** Dario Tainer, AIA; Thom Green; Rick Proppe; Dan Marshall; Jorge Reyes; Carole Post **SIZE:** 3,500 square feet **EMPLOYEES:** 15 **PHOTOGRAPHER:** Wayne E. Cable

CARPETING: Bigelow, Design Tex; **FURNITURE:** Atelier International Inc. (conference table), Geiger International (conference seating, office desk, office credenza), ICF (office side chair), Herman Miller "Equa" (workstation seating), Gianni Inc. (work desks, reception desk wood, conference ledge), Quadrex International (storage, granite); **FABRIC:** Lee Jofa; **MURALS:** Clark Ellithorpe; **LIGHTING:** Atelier International Inc., Ron Rezek, Artemide.

Directory

OFFICES

ACKERMAN MCQUEEN
320 South Boston Boulevard
Suite 1200
Tulsa, Oklahoma 74103
Tel: (918) 582-6200
Fax: (918) 582-4512

AIRTOUCH COMMUNICATIONS
One California Street
San Francisco,
California 94111
Tel: (415) 658-2207

THE AMERICAN TRADE CENTER
2 Berezhkovskaya Nab
Moscow
Russia

ANSHEN + ALLEN
5055 Wilshire Boulevard
9th Floor
Los Angeles, California 90036
Tel: (213) 525-0500
Fax: (213) 525-0955

APPLE COMPUTER, INC.
3 Infinite Loop
Cupertino, California 95014
Tel: (408) 996-1010
Fax: (408) 974-8896

APPLICAZIONI SRL
Via Guizzetti 73
Dosson di Casier - TV 31030
Italy
Tel: 39 422 490 611

ARNALL, GOLDEN & GREGORY
One Atlantic Center
1201 West Peachtree Street
NW, Suite 2800
Atlanta, Georgia 30309
Tel: (404) 873-8700
Fax: (404) 873-8501

AXIOM BUSINESS CONSULTING
539 Bryant Street
San Francisco,
California 94107
Tel: (415) 546-6800

BAKER & MCKENZIE
130 East Randolph
Chicago, Illinois 60601
Tel: (312) 861-8000
Fax: (312) 861-2898

BANK OF AMERICA
231 South LaSalle Street
Chicago, Illinois 60697
Tel: (312) 923-0300

BENNETT LOWRY CORPORATION
22 West 21st Street, 12th Floor
New York, New York 10010
Tel: (212) 989-1313
Fax: (212) 989-8384

BETSEY JOHNSON SHOWROOM
498 Seventh Avenue, 21st Floor
New York, New York 10018
Tel: (212) 244-0843
Fax: (212) 244-0866

BLACKROCK FINANCIAL
MANAGEMENT
65 Liberty Street
New York, New York 10005
Tel: (212) 754-5300

CENTRAL BANK OF CHINA
345 Park Avenue
New York, New York 10022
Tel: (914) 738-6300
Fax: (914) 738-6377

COCA-COLA ENTERPRISES, INC.
2500 Windy Ridge Parkway
Marietta, Georgia 30339
Tel: (404) 989-3051
Fax: (404) 989-3062

COREGIS CORPORATION
181 West Madison
Chicago, Illinois 60602
Tel: (312) 849-5000

CREDIT LYONNAIS
515 South Flower Street
Los Angeles, California 90071
Tel: (213) 627-3725
Fax: (213) 623-8067

DANIEL E. SNYDER
ARCHITECT, P.C.
216 East Gaston Street
Savannah, Georgia 31401
Tel: (912) 238-0410
Fax: (912) 238-5529

DESIGN COLLECTIVE
INCORPORATED
222 2nd Avenue North
Nashville, Tennessee 37201
Tel: (615) 242-7382
Fax: (615) 254-4613

ERNST & YOUNG LLP
GREAT LAKES MANAGEMENT
CONSULTING
1660 West 2nd Street
Suite 1200
Cleveland, Ohio 44113
Tel: (216) 861-5000

ESEO FEDERAL CREDIT UNION
636 NE 41st Street
Oklahoma City,
Oklahoma 73105
Tel: (405) 427-3654
Fax: (405) 427-1036

FALLON MCELLIGOTT
DUFFY, INC.
901 Marquette Avenue
Minneapolis, Minnesota 55402
Tel: (612) 332-2445

FX/MORNING STUDIOS
212 Fifth Avenue
New York, New York 10010
Tel: (310) 369-3075
Fax: (310) 369-3779

G. H. BASS & CO.
1414 Avenue of the Americas
New York, New York 10019
Tel: (207) 791-4440

HANLEY-WOOD, INC.
One Thomas Circle, NW
Washington, D.C. 20005
Tel: (202) 452-0800
Fax: (202) 785-1974

HANNA BARBERA PRODUCTIONS
3400 Cahuenga Boulevard
Los Angeles, California 90068
Tel: (213) 851-5000

JOHNS & GORMAN FILMS
5620 Hollywood Boulevard
Los Angeles, California 90028
Tel: (213) 467-4400
Fax: (213) 467-8780

LAW OFFICE
V.F. Crispi, 89
I-00187 Rome
Italy
Tel: 06-6780 177
Fax: 06-6790 360

MARTIN/BASTIAN
COMMUNICATIONS
105 5th Avenue South
Minneapolis, Minnesota 55401
Tel: (612) 375-0055
Fax: (612) 342-2348

MCI COMMUNICATIONS
CORPORATION
1800 Pennsylvania Avenue NW
Washington, D.C. 20036
Tel: (202) 872-1600
Fax: (202) 887-2178

MONTROY ANDERSEN
DESIGN GROUP
432 Park Avenue South
10th Floor
New York, New York 10016
Tel: (212) 481-5900
Fax: (212) 481-7481

THE MORRIS GENERAL AGENCY
700 Cedar Lake Boulevard
Oklahoma City,
Oklahoma 74113
Tel: (405) 478-7700
Fax: (405) 478-1205

NATIONAL MINORITY
AIDS COUNCIL
1931 13th Street, NW
Washington, D.C. 20009-4432
Tel: (202) 483-6622
Fax: (202) 483-1135

PORTER/NOVELLI
1120 Connecticut Avenue NW
Suite 1100
Washington, D.C. 20036
Tel: (202) 973-5800
Fax: (202) 973-5858

PUTNAM INVESTMENTS
One Post Office Square
Boston, Massachusetts 02109
Tel: (617) 292-1000

SWID POWELL
55 West 13th Street
New York, New York 10010
Tel: (212) 633-6699
Fax: (212) 633-0030

TAINER ASSOCIATES, LTD.
445 West Erie, Suite 201
Chicago, Illinois 60610
Tel: (312) 951-1656
Fax: (312) 951-8773

THE TIMBERLAND
  COMPANY, INC.
200 Domain Drive
Stratham,
New Hampshire 03885
Tel: (603) 772-9500
Fax: (603) 773-1640

TSUI DESIGN AND RESEARCH, INC.
4065 Emery Street
Emeryville, California 94608
Tel: (510) 658-8989
Fax: (510) 658-7289

UNITED MEDIA
200 Madison Avenue
New York, New York 10016
Tel: (212) 293-8706
Fax: (212) 293-8717

WARNER INTERNATIONAL
  CHANNELS
4000 West Alameda, 6th Floor
Burbank, California 91522
Tel: (818) 954-6166
Fax: (818) 954-6860

WIRED VENTURES LTD.
520 3rd Street, 4th Floor
San Francisco,
California 94107
Tel: (415) 222-6200
Fax: (415) 222-6209

WORTH MAGAZINE
575 Lexington Avenue
New York, New York 10022
Tel: (212) 223-3100
Fax: (212) 223-1597

ZIVKOVIC ASSOCIATES
  ARCHITECTS P.C.
100 Vandam Street, 5th Floor
New York, New York 10013
Tel: (212) 807-8577
Fax: (212) 807-9575

ARCHITECTS & DESIGNERS

ADD INC.
80 Prospect Street
Cambridge,
Massachusetts 02139
Tel: (617) 661-0165
Fax: (617) 661-7118

PAUL BENNETT
22 West 21st Street, 12th Floor
New York, New York 10010
Tel: (212) 989-1313
Fax: (212) 989-8384

CARMEN NORDSTEN
IGONDA DESIGN INC.
8900 Melrose Avenue #201
Los Angeles, California 90069
Tel: (310) 246-0993
Fax: (310) 246-0614

COE DESIGN ARCHITECTURE
2154 Westwood Boulevard
Los Angeles, California 90025
Tel: (310) 441-2772
Fax: (310) 441-2774

CORE
1010 Wisconsin Avenue #405
Washington, D.C. 20007
Tel: (202) 466-6116
Fax: (202) 466-6235

DANIEL E. SNYDER
  ARCHITECT, P.C.
216 East Gaston Street
Savannah, Georgia 31401
Tel: (912) 238-0410
Fax: (912) 238-5529

DESIGN COLLECTIVE
  INCORPORATED
222 2nd Avenue North
Nashville, Tennessee 37201
Tel: (615) 242-7382
Fax: (615) 254-4613

ELKUS/MANFREDI ARCHITECTS LTD.
530 Atlantic Avenue
Boston, Massachusetts 02210
Tel: (617) 426-1300
Fax: (617) 426-7502

RAND ELLIOTT
Elliott + Associates Architects
35 Harrison Avenue
Oklahoma City,
Oklahoma 73104
Tel: (405) 232-9554
Fax: (405) 232-9997

GRISWOLD, HECKEK & KELLY
  ASSOCIATES, INC. (GHK)
55 West Wacker Drive
Chicago, Illinois 60601
Tel: (312) 263-6605
Fax: (312) 263-1228

GRISWOLD, HECKEK & KELLY
  ASSOCIATES, INC. (GHK)
One Faneuil Hall Marketplace
Boston, Massachusetts 02109
Tel: (617) 723-2180
Fax: (617) 723-6308

HCA PARTNERS, INC.
54 West Green Street
Pasadena, California 91105
Tel: (818) 796-3876

HELLMUTH, OBATA & KASSEBAUM
71 Stevenson Street
San Francisco,
California 94105
Tel: (415) 243-0555
Fax: (415) 882-7763

HLW INTERNATIONAL LLP
115 Fifth Avenue
New York, New York 10003
Tel: (212) 353-4600
Fax: (212) 353-4666

HOLEY ASSOCIATES
1045 Sansome Street, Suite 204
San Francisco,
California 94111
Tel: (415) 397-3131
Fax: (415) 397-2857

GARY L. JOHNSON
603 Summit Avenue
St. Paul, Minnesota 55102
Tel: (612) 222-7182

KING-MIRANDA ASSOCIATI
Via Forcella, 3
20144 Milan
Italy
Tel: 39 2 8394963
Fax: 39 2 8360735

MANCINI DUFFY
Two World Trade Center
  Suite 2110
New York, New York 10048
Tel: (212) 938-1260
Fax: (212) 938-1267

MEKUS JOHNSON INC.
455 East Illinois
Chicago, Illinois 60611
Tel: (312) 321-0778
Fax: (312) 661-0980

MONTROY ANDERSEN
  DESIGN GROUP
432 Park Avenue South
  10th Floor
New York, New York 10016
Tel: (212) 481-5900
Fax: (212) 481-7481

PARSONS + FERNANDEZ-
  CASTELEIRO, PC
62 White Street
New York, New York 10013
Tel: (212) 431-4310
Fax: (212) 431-4496

PAUL GATES ARCHITECT
155 Sixth Avenue
  Suite 1202
New York, New York 10013
Tel: (212) 675-0790
Fax: (212) 206-0122

SCHWEITZER BIM
5541 West Washington
  Boulevard
Los Angeles, California 90016
Tel: (213) 936-6163
Fax: (213) 936-5327

STEPHEN SILLS & ASSOCIATES
30 East 67th Street
New York, New York 10021
Tel: (212) 988-1636

STEVENS & WILKINSON
  INTERIORS INC.
100 Peachtree Street
Atlanta, Georgia 30303
Tel: (404) 522-8888
Fax: (404) 521-6204

STUDIOS ARCHITECTURE
1133 Connecticut Avenue NW
Washington, D.C. 20036
Tel: (202) 736-5900
Fax: (202) 736-5959

STUDIOS ARCHITECTURE
99 Green Street
San Francisco,
California 94111
Tel: (415) 398-7575
Fax: (415) 398-3829

TAINER ASSOCIATES, LTD.
445 West Erie, Suite 201
Chicago, Illinois 60610
Tel: (312) 951-1656
Fax: (312) 951-8773

TARIK CURRIMBHOY
 DESIGN & ARCHITECTURE
17 East 16th Street
New York, New York 10003
Tel: (212) 647-0920
Fax: (212) 647-9730

TRANSIT DESIGN
Via E. Morosini, 17
I-00153 Rome
Italy
Tel: 06-5899 848
Fax: 06-5898 431

TSUI DESIGN AND RESEARCH, INC.
4065 Emery Street
Emeryville, California 94608
Tel: (510) 658-8989
Fax: (510) 658-7289

VOA ASSOCIATES INCORPORATED
224 South Michigan Avenue
 Suite 1400
Chicago, Illinois 60604
Tel: (312) 554-1400
Fax: (312) 554-1412

THE WHEELER GROUP
Amy L. Kleppe
James E. Young
701 Fourth Avenue South
Minneapolis, Minnesota 55415
Tel: (612) 339-1102
Fax: (612) 337-5040

ZIVKOVIC ASSOCIATES
 ARCHITECTS P.C.
100 Vandam Street, 5th Floor
New York, New York 10013
Tel: (212) 807-8577
Fax: (212) 807-9575

PHOTOGRAPHERS

ASSASSI PRODUCTIONS
P. O. Box 3651
Santa Barbara,
California 93130
Tel: (805) 682-2158
Fax: (805) 682-1185

RICHARD BARNES
1403 Shotwell Street
San Francisco,
California 94110
Tel: (415) 550-1023

TOM BONNER
1201 Abbot Kinney Boulevard
Venice, California 90291
Tel: (310) 396-7125
Fax: (310) 396-4792

ANDREW BUSH
755 North Lafayette
Park Place #2
Los Angeles, California 90026
Tel: (213) 484-0367
Fax: (214) 413-6919

WAYNE E. CABLE
Cable Studios
312 North Carpenter Street
Chicago, Illinois 60607
Tel: (312) 226-6995

PAUL GATES
155 Sixth Avenue, Suite 1202
New York, New York 10013
Tel: (212) 675-0790
Fax: (212) 206-0122

JANOS GRAPOW
Via Monti Pariou 21/A
Rome
Italy
Tel: 06-3244 831

STEVE HALL
Hedrich-Blessing
11 West Illinois Avenue
Chicago, Illinois 60610
Tel: (312) 321-1151
Fax: (312) 321-1165

MICHAEL HOUGHTON
StudiOhio
55 East Spring Street
Columbus, Ohio 43215
Tel: (614) 224-4885
Fax: (614) 224-8317

MARCO LORENZETTI
Korab/Hedrich-Blessing
5051 Beach Road
Troy, Michigan 48099
Tel: (810) 952-1970

RICHARD MANDELKORN
65 Beaver Pond Road
Lincoln, Massachusetts 01773
Tel: (617) 259-3310
Fax: (617) 259-3312

BRUCE MARTIN
17 Tudor Street
Cambridge,
Massachusetts 02139
Tel: (617) 492-8009

CHAS MCGRATH
347 Corlano Court
Santa Rosa, California 95404
Tel: (707) 664-9980
Fax: (707) 664-9981

JON MILLER
Hedrich-Blessing
11 West Illinois Avenue
Chicago, Illinois 60610
Tel: (312) 321-1151
Fax: (312) 321-1165

MICHAEL MORAN
245 Mulberry Street #14
New York, New York 10012
Tel: (212) 226-2596
Fax: (212) 219-1566

JERRY NELSON
3230 Kyle Avenue North
Golden Valley,
Minnesota 55442
Tel: (612) 522-0222

PETER PAIGE
269 Parkside Road
Harrington Park,
New Jersey 07640
Tel: (201) 767-3150
Fax: (201) 767-9263

ASHLEY RANSON
Box 151
260 Adelaide Street East
Toronto, Ontario M5A 1N1
Canada
Tel: (416) 346-2658

TIM RHOAD
420 Jefferson Street
Savannah, Georgia 31401
Tel: (912) 238-0422

BOB SHIMER
Hedrich-Blessing
11 West Illinois Avenue
Chicago, Illinois 60610
Tel: (312) 321-1151
Fax: (312) 321-1165

EUGENE TSUI
Tsui Design and Research, Inc.
4065 Emery Street
Emeryville, California 94608
Tel: (510) 658-8989
Fax: (510) 658-7289

PETER VANDERWARKER
28 Prince Street
West Newton,
Massachusetts 02165
Tel: (617) 964-2728

PAUL WARCHOL
133 Mulberry Street #6S
New York, New York 10013
Tel: (212) 431-3461
Fax: (212) 274-1953

DANA WHEELOCK
800 Washington Avenue North
Minneapolis, Minnesota 55401
Tel: (612) 333-5110
Fax: (612) 338-0806

TOSHI YOSHIMI
4030 Camero Drive
Los Angeles, California 90027
Tel: (213) 660-9043
Fax: (213) 660-2497

ANDREA ZANI
Via Crema, 29
20135 Milan
Italy
Tel: 39 2 55 18 98 60

WADE ZIMMERMAN
9 East 97th Street
New York, New York 10029
Tel: (212) 427-8784
Fax: (212) 427-3526

Index

A C K N O W L E D G M E N T S

My sincere appreciation and thanks to the interior designers and architects whose extraordinary work has inspired this book. And whose creativity has excited and sustained me since that damp December day when I first looked through their many remarkable projects.

I thank the photographers whose superb work appears on these pages and am indebted for their generosity. Especially I thank Wade Zimmerman for his on-going search for new projects and keeping me in touch when I was living in Maine.

My appreciation to PBC International, Penny Sibal and the editorial and art staff, Deby Bennett, Daniela Graziose and Jennifer Moglia for their dedication and enthusiasm in making this book a reality.

And finally my love and thanks to my daughter Georgia who led our morning yoga sessions, supported my search for the right word, and made me laugh.